EXPLANATORY NOTES

CONSUMER RIGHTS ACT 2015

GRAN*GIS* UK Publishing

Adapted and published by GRANGIS (Grand Register Library).
Online: www.grangis.com
E-mail: contact@grangis.com

In this version:
ISBN: 979-8-88559-041-9

Note: This is the original version (as it was originally enacted). Title, sub-title and the generated date is as marked on the pages.

These notes refer to the Consumer Rights Act 2015 (c.15)

EXPLANATORY NOTES

CONSUMER RIGHTS ACT 2015

What statutory rights are there under a goods contract?

Section 9: Goods to be of satisfactory quality

Section 10: Goods to be fit for particular purpose

Section 11: Goods to be as described

Section 12: Other pre-contract information included in contract

Section 13: Goods to match a sample

Section 14: Goods to match a model seen or examined

Section 15: Installation as part of conformity of the goods with the contract

Section 16: Goods not conforming to contract if digital content does not conform

Section 17: Trader to have right to supply the goods etc

Section 18: No other requirement to treat term about quality or fitness as included

What remedies are there if statutory rights under a goods contract are not met?

Section 19: Consumer's rights to enforce terms about goods

Section 20: Right to reject

Section 21: Partial rejection of goods

Section 22: Time limit for short-term right to reject

Section 23: Right to repair or replacement

Section 24: Right to price reduction or final right to reject

Other rules about remedies under goods contracts

Section 25: Delivery of wrong quantity

Section 26: Instalment deliveries

Section 27: Consignation, or payment into court, in Scotland

Other rules about goods contracts

Section 28: Delivery of goods

Section 29: Passing of risk

Section 30: Goods offered with a guarantee

These notes refer to the Consumer Rights Act 2015 (c.15) which received Royal Assent on 26 March 2015

CONSUMER RIGHTS ACT 2015

EXPLANATORY NOTES

INTRODUCTION

1. These explanatory notes relate to the Consumer Rights Act 2015 which received Royal Assent on 26 March 2015. They have been prepared by the Department for Business, Innovation and Skills in order to assist the reader in understanding the Act. They do not form part of the Act and have not been endorsed by Parliament.

2. The notes need to be read in conjunction with the Act. They are not, and are not meant to be, a comprehensive description of the Act. So where a section or part of a section does not seem to require any explanation or comments, none is given.

SUMMARY AND BACKGROUND

3. The Consumer Rights Act 2015 sets out a framework that consolidates in one place key consumer rights covering contracts for goods, services, digital content and the law relating to unfair terms in consumer contracts. In addition, the Act introduces easier routes for consumers and small and medium sized enterprises ("SMEs") to challenge anti-competitive behaviour through the Competition Appeal Tribunal ("CAT"). The Act clarifies the maximum penalties that the regulator of premium rate services can impose on non-compliant and rogue operators. It also consolidates enforcers' powers as listed in Schedule 5 to investigate potential breaches of consumer law and clarifies that certain enforcers (Trading Standards) can operate across local authority boundaries. It will also give the civil courts and public enforcers greater flexibility to take the most appropriate action for consumers when dealing with breaches or potential breaches of consumer law. Additionally, it changes the way in which judges are able to sit as chairs in the CAT; and imposes a duty on letting agents to publish their fees and other information. Further, the Act expands the list of higher education providers which are required to join the higher education complaints handling scheme, and includes certain requirements relating to resale of tickets for recreational, sporting and cultural events.

4. The Act is in three Parts:

- Consumer contracts for goods, digital content and services;
- Unfair terms; and
- Miscellaneous and general, including investigatory powers; amendment of the Weights and Measures (Packaged Goods) Regulations 2006; enhanced consumer measures and other enforcement under the Enterprise Act 2002; clarification of the maximum penalties that the regulator of premium rate services can impose on non-compliant and rogue operators; private actions in competition law; a change in the way in which judges are able to sit as chairs in the CAT; a duty on letting agents to publicise fees and other information; expansion of the list of higher education providers which are required to join the higher education complaints handling scheme; and certain requirements relating to resale of tickets for recreational, sporting and cultural events.

Background

5. There is general agreement across business and consumer groups that the existing UK consumer law is unnecessarily complex. It is fragmented and, in places, unclear, for example where the law has not kept up with technological change or lacks precision or where it is couched in legalistic language. There are also overlaps and inconsistencies between changes made by virtue of implementing European Union ("EU") legislation alongside unamended pre-existing UK legislation.

6. The law that protects consumers when they enter into contracts has developed piecemeal over time. Initially it was the courts that recognised that a person buying goods has certain clear and justified, but sometimes unspoken, expectations. The courts developed a body of case law which gave buyers rights when these expectations were not met. This case law was then made into legislation that protected buyers when buying goods, originally in the Sale of Goods Act 1893, updated by the Sale of Goods Act 1979 ("SGA"). These rights were then extended by the introduction of the Supply of Goods and Services Act 1982 ("SGSA") to cover the situations when goods were provided other than by sale (for example when someone hires goods). The SGSA also covers (in relation to England, Wales and Northern Ireland) certain protections for the recipients of services supplied by traders. Legislation setting out rules on unfairness in contract terms was established domestically in the Unfair Contract Terms Act 1977 ("UCTA"). These pieces of legislation currently cover more than just consumer contracts but certain of their provisions offer extra protection to consumers (as opposed to other types of buyers).

7. The EU has also legislated to protect consumers and so the UK legislation has been amended to incorporate this European legislation; sometimes this has been implemented in domestic law without resolving inconsistencies or overlaps.

8. The relevant domestic law is currently mainly contained in the following legislation:

- Supply of Goods (Implied Terms) Act 1973
- Sale of Goods Act 1979
- Supply of Goods and Services Act 1982
- Sale and Supply of Goods Act 1994
- Sale and Supply of Goods to Consumers Regulations 2002
- Unfair Contract Terms Act 1977
- Unfair Terms in Consumer Contracts Regulations 1999
- Unfair Terms in Consumer Contracts (Amendment) Regulations 2001
- Competition Act 1998
- Enterprise Act 2002

9. The European Directives implemented in the Act are:

- Directive 99/44/EC of the European Parliament and of the Council on certain aspects of the sale of consumer goods and associated guarantees;
- Directive 93/13/EEC of the Council on unfair terms in consumer contracts;
- Some provisions of Directive 2011/83/EU of the European Parliament and of the Council on consumer rights. See sections 11, 12, 36, 37 and 50 in relation to the enforcement of information requirements and also see paragraph 11 below. See also section 28 in relation to default rules for the delivery of goods, and section 29 regarding the passing of risk in goods.

10. In addition, the Act implements some provisions (in respect of enforcement) of:

- Regulation (EC) No. 2006/2004 of the European Parliament and of the Council on cooperation between national authorities responsible for the enforcement of consumer protection laws;
- Regulation (EC) No. 765/2008 of the European Parliament and of the Council setting out the requirements for accreditation and market surveillance relating to the marketing of products;
- Directive 2001/95/EC of the European Parliament and of the Council on general product safety; and
- Directive 98/27/EC of the European Parliament and of the Council on injunctions for the protection of consumers' interests.

Wider reforms to the consumer legislation framework

11. In addition to the Act, the Consumer Contracts (Information, Cancellation and Additional Charges) Regulations 2013 implement Directive 2011/83/EU of the European Parliament and of the Council on consumer rights (commonly known as the Consumer Rights Directive ("CRD")) in regulations made under the European Communities Act 1972. These regulations came into force on 13 June 2014. However, a small number of the CRD's provisions are implemented in the Act, as indicated above. The CRD:

- for all contracts where a trader supplies goods, services or digital content to a consumer, requires that a trader must provide certain information (for example on the main characteristics of the goods, services and digital content) before the consumer is bound by the contract;
- specifies the consumer's cancellation rights (during so-called "cooling off periods") for goods, services and digital content contracts concluded at a distance or off premises; and
- introduces various measures aimed at protecting consumers from hidden charges once they have entered into a contract.

12. A consultation by the Department for Business Innovation and Skills ("BIS") in August 2012 sought views on implementing the CRD in particular highlighting those areas where the UK had some flexibility in the way it might be applied[1]. A Government response was published in August 2013. Part of the CRD was implemented early as the Consumer Rights (Payment Surcharges) Regulations 2012, and the remainder was implemented with effect from 13 June 2014 as the Consumer Contracts (Information, Cancellation and Additional Charges) Regulations 2013.

13. In developing proposals for the Consumer Rights Act 2015, the Government has taken into account the definitions and measures contained within the CRD and, as far as appropriate, has made the Act consistent with the CRD, with the intention of achieving overall a simple, coherent framework of consumer legislation.

14. The Government has also implemented the majority of the recommendations made by the Law Commission and Scottish Law Commission ("the Law Commissions") following their findings that the law surrounding consumer rights to redress following misleading or aggressive practices by traders is fragmented, complex and unclear[2]. The Consumer Protection (Amendment) Regulations 2014[3] amend the Consumer Protection from Unfair Trading Regulations 2008 ("CPRs") and, as such, this reform did not need to be introduced within the Consumer Rights Act 2015. The new rights came

---

1 A consultation on implementing the Consumer Rights Directive, BIS, August 2012
2 The Law Commission No.332/The Scottish Law Commission No.226, March 2012
3 http://www.legislation.gov.uk/uksi/2014/870/contents/made

into force on 1 October 2014 and give consumers the right to unwind a contract or payment, or receive a discount on the price paid, if they are subjected to misleading or aggressive practices. The Government published its response to its consultation on the draft regulations on 2 April 2014[4].

Advice and consultations

15. The University of East Anglia concluded in 2008 that the UK consumer protection regime had two key weaknesses – uneven enforcement and excessively complex law[5]. A call for evidence in the Consumer Law Review in 2008 revealed strong support across the board for consolidating consumer legislation, making it clearer and more accessible[6]. Respondents highlighted a number of benefits that a rewrite would bring – removing discrepancies and inconsistencies, greater use of plain English, greater awareness of rights, remedies and obligations, greater flexibility, future proofing and aiding business growth.

16. A number of consultations and academic research papers over several years have examined proposals that form part of this Act. A single Government response to BIS consultations between March and November 2012 and a report by the Law Commissions of March 2013 (detailed below) was published alongside a draft Bill with accompanying explanatory notes. The draft Bill was scrutinised by the House of Commons Business Innovation and Skills Committee. The Committee published a report in December 2013[7].

Part 1

17. The Davidson report in 2006, which examined the transposition of European Directives into domestic law, concluded that UK law on the sale of goods was unnecessarily complex[8]. The Law Commissions consulted on potential changes to the law on remedies for faulty goods and made recommendations in 2009[9]. Professors G. Howells and C. Twigg-Flesner examined the law on goods and services in 2010 and made recommendations to BIS on how the law could be clarified and simplified[10]. Also in 2010, Professor Bradgate reported to BIS on the uncertainty in current law around consumer rights to quality for digital content products[11]. Following these various reports, BIS consulted from July to October 2012 on proposals to clarify consumer rights in goods, services and digital content[12].

Part 2

18. Legislation on unfair contract terms is contained in the UCTA, which currently applies to contracts between businesses and between consumers but contains some particular rules about business to consumer contracts. It makes some terms in contracts automatically non-binding and subjects others to a test of reasonableness. The Unfair Terms in Consumer Contract Regulations 1999 ("UTCCRs") enable consumers to challenge most non-negotiated terms of a contract on the grounds that they are unfair. There are certain terms that cannot be assessed for fairness: terms that relate to the definition of the main subject matter of the contract and those that relate to the adequacy of the price or remuneration as against the goods or services supplied in exchange. These are known as "exempt terms". In August 2002 the Law Commissions issued a consultation proposing a unified law on unfair contracts terms

---

4 https://www.gov.uk/government/consultations/protecting-consumers-from-misleading-and-aggressive-selling
5 Benchmarking the performance of the UK framework supporting consumer empowerment through comparison against relevant international comparator countries, a study for BERR by UEA, 2008
6 Consumer Law Review: Summary of Responses, BIS, 2009
7 Draft Consumer Rights Bill; sixth report of session 2013-2014
8 Davidson Report, HM Treasury, 2006
9 The Law Commission No.317/The Scottish Law Commission No.216, 2009
10 Consolidation and simplification of UK consumer law, BIS, 2010
11 Consumer rights in digital products, BIS, 2010
12 Enhancing consumer confidence by clarifying consumer law, BIS, 2012

and, in February 2005, they issued a report setting out detailed recommendations, which was published alongside a draft Bill[13]. These recommendations were not taken forward at the time. However, in May 2012 the Parliamentary Under-Secretary of State for Employment Relations, Consumer and Postal Affairs, Norman Lamb MP, asked the Law Commissions to look again at unifying a regime on unfair terms in consumer contracts, focusing on the exempt terms. From July to October 2012 the Law Commissions sought views on a discussion paper on revised proposals for the exempt terms and made recommendations to BIS in March 2013[14] concerning terms in consumer contracts.

Part 3

19. There are a number of pieces of legislation that set out rights and duties on traders. To ensure effective enforcement of these rights and duties, enforcers such as local weights and measures authorities (known as "Trading Standards") and other regulators (such as the Competition and Markets Authority ("CMA")) have powers to investigate compliance. These investigatory powers are usually set out in the individual pieces of legislation creating the rights or duties and whilst largely similar, have some differences between them. In March 2012, BIS published a consultation on consolidating and modernising enforcement officers' investigatory powers into a generic set. It also consulted on removing the barriers to trading standards operating efficiently[15]. Additionally, views were also sought on reducing burdens on business by introducing certain safeguards on the use of these powers, such as requiring officers to give reasonable notice of routine visits, unless there are good reasons for them to be unannounced.

20. In November 2012, BIS published a consultation paper on extending the range of remedies available to courts when public enforcers apply to them for enforcement orders under Part 8 of the Enterprise Act 2002 ("EA")[16].

21. Research by the OFT showed that businesses view the present approach to private actions by consumers and businesses as one of the least effective aspects of the UK competition regime. BIS consulted on measures to make it easier and simpler for businesses and consumers to challenge anti-competitive behaviour in April 2012 and Government published its response in January 2013[17].

Structure of the Act

22. The Act consists of three parts and ten Schedules. The general arrangement of the Act is as follows:

Part	*Summary*
Part 1	• Sets out the standards that goods must meet. • Consolidates and aligns the currently inconsistent remedies available to consumers for goods supplied under different contract types, such as sale, work and materials, conditional sale or hire purchase. • Sets a time period of 30 days in which consumers can reject substandard goods and be entitled to a full refund. • Limits the number of repairs or replacements of substandard goods before traders must offer some money back.

13 The Law Commission No.292/The Scottish Law Commission No.199, 2005
14 Unfair terms in consumer contracts – advice to BIS, The Law Commission & The Scottish Law Commission, 2013
15 Enhancing consumer confidence through effective enforcement, BIS, March 2012
16 Civil enforcement remedies – consultation on extending the range of remedies available to public enforcers of consumer law, BIS, November 2012
17 Private actions in competition law: a consultation on options for reform, BIS, April 2012 and a government response, BIS, January 2013

Part	**Summary**
	• Sets limits on the extent to which traders may reduce the level of refund (where goods are not rejected initially) to take account of the use of the goods the consumer has had up to that point. • Introduces a new category of digital content. • Introduces tailored quality rights for digital content. • Introduces tailored remedies if the digital content rights are not met. • Introduces a new statutory right that if a trader provides information in relation to a service, and the consumer takes this information into account, the service must comply with that information. • Introduces new statutory remedies when things go wrong with a service. • Makes it clear that consumers can always request these rights and remedies when a trader supplies a service to them.
Part 2 including Schedules 2, 3 and 4	• Consolidates the legislation governing unfair contract terms in relation to consumer contracts, which currently is found in two separate pieces of legislation, into one place, removes anomalies and overlapping provisions in relation to consumer contracts. • Makes clearer the circumstances when the price or subject matter of the contract cannot be considered for fairness and in particular makes clear that to avoid being considered for fairness those terms must be transparent and prominent. • Clarifies the role of and extends the indicative list of terms which may be regarded as unfair (the so-called 'grey list').
Part 3 including Schedules 5, 6, 7, 8, 9 and 10	• Consolidates and simplifies the investigatory powers of consumer law enforcers in relation to the listed legislation and sets them out in one place as a generic set[18]. • Clarifies the law so that trading standards are able to work across local authority boundaries as simply and efficiently as possible. • Introduces new powers for public enforcers to seek, through applying to the civil courts: — Redress for consumers who have been disadvantaged by breaches of consumer law; — Remedies from traders who have breached consumer law to improve their compliance and reduce the likelihood of future breaches, and/or — Remedies to give consumers more information so they can exercise greater choice and help improve the functioning of the market for consumers and other businesses. • Includes a power for the Secretary of State to extend the use of the enhanced consumer measures to private designated enforcers providing certain conditions are met and subject to safeguards on their use. • Clarifies the maximum penalties that the regulator of premium rate services can impose on non-compliant and rogue operators.

18 Some specific powers contained in weights and measures and product safety legislation will be retained alongside the new generic set

Part	***Summary***
	• Establishes the CAT as a major venue for competition actions in the UK. • Introduces a limited opt-out collective actions regime, with safeguards, for competition law. • Promotes ADR for competition cases. • Changes the way in which judges are able to sit as chairs in the Competition Appeals Tribunal (CAT). • Imposes a duty on letting agents to publicise fees and a statement of whether or not they are a member of a client money protection scheme and which redress scheme they have joined. • Expands the list of higher education providers which are required to join the higher education complaints handling scheme. • Includes certain requirements relating to resale of tickets for recreational, sporting and cultural events.

Impact on existing legislation

23. The Act brings together key consumer rights from all the enactments listed in paragraph 8 above. It will harmonise existing provisions to give a single approach where appropriate.

24. The provisions in the existing legislation listed below which cover trader to consumer contracts only will be repealed. The provisions which relate to other types of contract (for example contracts between businesses) will remain in the existing legislation.

Supply of Goods (Implied Terms) Act 1973	For business to consumer contracts the provisions of the Supply of Goods (Implied Terms) Act 1973 ("SGITA") will be replaced by the Consumer Rights Act 2015. It will be amended so that it covers business to business contracts and consumer to consumer contracts only.
Sale of Goods Act 1979	For business to consumer contracts this will mainly be replaced by the Consumer Rights Act 2015 but some provisions of SGA will still apply, for example, rules which are applicable to all contracts of sale of goods (as defined by that Act – essentially these are sales of goods for money), regarding matters such as when property in goods passes. The SGA will still apply to business to business contracts and to consumer to consumer contracts.
Supply of Goods and Services Act 1982	For business to consumer contracts, this Act's provisions will be replaced by the Consumer Rights Act 2015. The SGSA will be amended so that it covers business to business contracts and consumer to consumer contracts only.
Sale and Supply of Goods Act 1994	This Act amended the SGA and the SGSA and as such will be superseded by provisions

18 Some specific powers contained in weights and measures and product safety legislation will be retained alongside the new generic set

	in the Consumer Rights Act 2015 for business to consumer contracts.
Sale and Supply of Goods to Consumers Regulations 2002	These will be replaced by provisions in the Consumer Rights Act 2015.
Unfair Contract Terms Act 1977	In respect of business to consumer contracts the Act's provisions will be replaced by the Consumer Rights Act 2015. The UCTA will be amended so that it covers business to business and consumer to consumer contracts only.
Unfair Terms in Consumer Contracts Regulations 1999	These will be replaced by the Consumer Rights Act 2015.

Territorial extent and application

25. The Act extends to England and Wales, Scotland and Northern Ireland as described below.

26. Parts 1 to 3 largely extend to the whole of the UK. Some of Part 3 does not apply to Scotland or Northern Ireland because of the differences in the law. For example, the provision relating to the Competition Appeal Tribunal issuing injunctions in private actions does not apply to Scotland, and some of the legislation which Part 3 proposes to amend does not extend to Scotland or Northern Ireland, e.g. the Sunday Trading Act 1994. Chapter 3 of Part 3 (duty on letting agents to publicise fees) extends only to England and Wales, and applies in relation to the fees charged by agents in the course of the letting and management of privately rented property in England and Wales. However, the requirement for letting agents to publicise whether or not they are a member of a client money protection scheme and which redress scheme they have joined applies only to England. The obligation to expand the requirement to join the complaints handling scheme in higher education applies to England and Wales on the basis that the original legislation extends to England and Wales only.

Which country's law governs the contract?

27. European Regulation EC 593/2008 on the law applicable to contractual obligations sets out the rules as to which country's law applies to consumer contracts. It is known as the "Rome I Regulation". It confirms that it is open to a consumer and a trader to choose the law of any country to govern their contract. Where they do not choose, if a trader pursues its activities in or directs its activities to the UK, (whether the trader is in the UK or not) and the contract covers those activities, the Rome I Regulation provides that a contract with a consumer habitually living in the UK will be governed by UK law. Even if the consumer and trader do choose another country's law to govern their contract, the Rome I Regulation provides that where the trader pursues or directs its activities to the UK and the consumer is habitually resident in the UK, any UK protections that parties cannot contract out of under UK law (such as the key protections covered by this Act) will still apply. Depending on the circumstances, pursuing or directing activities might, for example, include having a website translated into English or with a '.uk' web address from which consumers in the UK can purchase goods, services or digital content in sterling.

28. Some of the provisions regarding goods and unfair terms will also apply in other circumstances, due to protections in the Directives from which these derive. See the notes on sections 32 and 74 below.

Transposition of EU Directives

29. The Act does not itself implement EU Directives for the first time with the exception of certain parts of Articles 5, 6 18, 20 and 23 of the CRD which are implemented in Part 1 as detailed above in paragraph 9. Other than this, the Act replaces earlier legislation which has implemented EU Directives, most of which is set out in paragraph 9 above.

COMMENTARY ON SECTIONS

Part 1: Consumer Contracts for Goods, Digital Content and Services

Section 1: Where Part 1 applies

30. The main purpose behind section 1 is to make clear the scope of Part 1 of the Act. Part 1 is concerned with contracts between a trader and a consumer under which a trader agrees to supply goods, digital content or services (or any combination of these) to a consumer. It does not matter whether the contract is written or oral or implied by the conduct of the trader and consumer, or a combination of these. This means that, for the Part to have effect, there must be a *contract* and the contract must be for a *trader* to supply goods, digital content or services to a *consumer*.

31. At its most basic level, for a contract to be formed under the law of England and Wales or Northern Ireland there needs to be an offer and acceptance (i.e. one party must express a willingness to contract on certain terms and the other party must agree to those terms); and there must be 'consideration,' which is to say that both sides must offer something to the other (e.g. money in return for goods). In Scots law there is no requirement for consideration but the parties' agreement must show an intention to be legally bound. As well as using words, a contract could be implied by conduct of the parties, for example, by jumping into a black cab and stating your destination, this conduct would be taken as an agreement that the taxi driver will take you to your destination and that you will pay a price for it.

32. *Subsections* (4) to (6) set out the position with regard to "mixed contracts". There are many examples of mixed contracts, for example contracts involving the supply of both goods and services (e.g. a car service where parts are fitted) or digital content and a service (e.g. supplying and installing anti-virus software). In such contracts, under the Act, the service element of the contract attracts service rights and remedies, the goods elements attract goods rights and remedies and the digital content elements attract the digital content rights and remedies. *Subsection* (3) therefore makes clear that, for such mixed contracts, it will be relevant to look at the rights and remedies for each element of the mixed contract. In most cases it will be relevant to look at the appropriate chapter of the Act (Chapter 2 for goods, 3 for digital content and 4 for services). Subsection (6) sets out that for particular mixed contracts (goods and installation services, and goods and digital content) it may also be relevant to look at sections 15 and 16.

33. *Subsection* (7) makes clear that consumer contracts are subject to provisions in Part 2 on unfair terms. In addition to the provisions of the Act, some provisions of SGA will continue to apply to trader-to-consumer contracts if they are contracts of sale as defined by SGA (essentially sales of goods for money). The provisions of SGA which continue to cover such contracts are:

- Sections 1-10 (certain provisions regarding formation of the contract)
- Section 11 with the exception of subsection (4) (when condition to be treated as a warranty)
- Sections 16-19, 20A and 20B (certain provisions regarding transfer of property)
- Sections 21-28 (provisions regarding transfer of title, duties of seller and buyer and payment and delivery being concurrent conditions)

- Section 29 with the exception of subsection (3) (rules about delivery)
- Section 34 (buyer's right of examining goods) – the consumer's remedies, if the goods are found to breach the statutory requirements under the Consumer Rights Act 2015, are still as set out in the Consumer Rights Act 2015
- Section 37 (buyer's liability for not taking delivery of goods)
- Part V (rights of unpaid seller against the goods)
- Sections 49-50 (seller's remedies)
- Section 57 (auction sales)
- Sections 60-62 (rights enforceable by action; interpretation and savings)

Section 2: ***Key definitions***

34. One of the policy objectives is to align, as far as possible, the definitions of certain key terms across the Act and other consumer law, such as the Consumer Contracts (Information, Cancellation and Additional Charges) Regulations 2013 which implement the CRD, to facilitate easier interpretation and clearer application of the law. These terms are "trader," "consumer," "goods" and "digital content". To ensure as much consistency as possible, the definitions of these key terms in the Act are based largely on the definitions within the CRD. This section sets out these key definitions in a section separate from the general interpretation section (section 59, which sets definitions of the other terms used in Part 1 of the Act that need definition) because they are vitally important to understanding the scope of the Act. 'Service' is also a key concept but is not defined by the Act; it was not defined in the SGSA.

35. *Subsection* (2) makes clear that a trader is a person acting for purposes relating to their trade, business, craft or profession. It makes clear that a trader acting through another person acting in the trader's name or on the trader's behalf, for example a trader which subcontracts part of a building contract or a company for which the employees make contracts with customers, is liable for proper performance of the contract. A "person" is not just a natural person but can also include companies, charities and arms of government (and the reference to a "person" can also include more than one person). So where these types of body are acting for purposes relating to their trade, business, craft or profession, they are caught by the definition of trader. *Subsection* (7) makes clear that a 'business' includes the activities of government departments and local and public authorities, which means that these bodies may therefore come within the definition of a trader. Not-for-profit organisations, such as charities, mutuals and cooperatives, may also come within the definition of a trader, for example, if a charity shop sells t-shirts or mugs, they would be acting within the meaning of trader.

36. Another key definition is the definition of "consumer". Firstly, a consumer must be an "individual" (that is, a natural person) – the Act's protection for consumers does not apply to small businesses or legally incorporated organisations (e.g. companies formed by groups of residents). If a group of consumers contracts for goods, services or digital content, they are not left without protection. For example if one consumer makes all the arrangements for a group to go to the theatre or to go on holiday, depending on the circumstances, each member of the group may be able to enforce their rights or the person who made the arrangements may have to enforce the rights on behalf of the group. The other main restriction on who is a consumer is that a consumer must be acting wholly or mainly outside their trade, business, craft or profession. This means, for example, that a person who buys a kettle for their home, works from home one day a week and uses it on the days when working from home would still be a consumer. Conversely a sole trader that operates from a private dwelling who buys a printer of which 95% of the use is for the purposes of the business, is not likely to be held to be a consumer (and therefore the rights in this Part will not protect that sole trader but they

would have to look to other legislation. For example, if the sole trader were buying goods, they would have to look to the SGA for protections about the quality of the goods).

37. *Subsection* (5) excludes (for some purposes) from the definition of consumers those acquiring second-hand goods at an auction which they have the opportunity to attend in person. This derives from the CSD (Article 1(3)), and the previous definition of "dealing as a consumer" under the UCTA. This exclusion applies to the Goods provisions in Chapter 2 only, other than those derived from the CRD (as the scope of the CRD is not subject to this exclusion) – its application is set out in *subsection* (6) and in the relevant sections.

38. *Subsection* (8) sets out another key definition: the meaning of "goods". This derives from Article 2(3) of the CRD. Essentially "goods" means anything physical which you can move ("any tangible moveable item"). Therefore, Chapter 2 of Part 1 of the Act (the goods Chapter) does not apply to purchases of immovable property such as land or a house. However, this subsection makes clear the meaning of goods can include certain utilities (water, gas and electricity) where they are put up for sale in a limited volume or set quantity. Examples of these are a gas cylinder, a bottle of water or a battery. Section 3 contains further provision on the scope of the contracts for goods covered by the Act.

39. The definition of digital content in *subsection* (9) is the same as the definition in the CRD (data produced and supplied in digital form). Digital content may be supplied on a tangible medium (in which case special rules apply) for example a DVD or software, on a computer or not, for example an e-book or music download. The creation of a category of digital content in this Act does not affect the treatment of digital content in any other legislation.

Chapter 2: ***Goods***

Summary and Background

40. This Chapter concerns contracts where a trader supplies goods to a consumer. It sets out:

- The rights a consumer has when a trader supplies goods under contract (the notes on section 1 explain how a contract may be formed). These are in effect contractual rights and if they are breached it is therefore a breach of contract;
- the statutory remedies to which the consumer is entitled if these rights are breached: namely a right to reject the goods within an initial period, a right to repair or replacement and a subsequent right to a reduction in the price (keeping the goods) or to reject the goods for a refund (subject to deduction for use in some cases);
- that the statutory remedies do not prevent the consumer claiming other remedies from the trader where they are available according to general contract law (e.g. damages); and
- that the trader cannot limit or exclude liability for breaches of the above rights, in most cases.

41. Currently (that is, until Chapter 2 and section 60 of the Act come into force), provisions relating to contracts to supply goods are contained within several different pieces of law. The SGA, the SGSA and the SGITA each contain provisions which apply, depending on the type of contract. Much of the legislation in place prior to the Act coming into force applies to recipients of goods (whether or not they are consumers), but some protections apply only to consumers.

Contract Type	*Description*	*Current applicable legislation (until Act comes into force)*
Sale	Supply of goods in exchange for money.	SGA
Conditional sale	Sale where the consumer pays in instalments and only obtains ownership of the goods when the final payment is made (or other conditions are satisfied), although the consumer may use the goods in the meantime.	SGA
Hire purchase	A contract of hire with an option or condition to buy at the end of the hiring period	SGITA
Barter or exchange	Where goods are exchanged for a consideration other than money	SGSA
Work and materials	Where the contract includes both the provision of a service and the supply of associated goods	SGSA
Hire of goods	A contract of hire where there is no intention that ownership of the goods will be transferred	SGSA

42. The current legislation provides that goods must meet certain standards – such as being of satisfactory quality, fit for purpose, corresponding to descriptions or samples by which they are supplied, and being free from third parties' rights - and provides that the trader must have the right to sell (or hire) the goods. These matters are treated in the current legislation as "implied terms" of a contract. Implied terms are terms that are not expressly set out in a contract (which are "express terms") but still form part of the contract.

43. The current legislation categorises these implied terms as "conditions" of the contract or "warranties" (save in relation to Scotland as this terminology does not apply in Scots law, but the legislation provides an equivalent effect). Most of the statutory implied terms are categorised as conditions, breach of which enables the consumer to choose either to treat the contract as terminated or to continue with the contract (i.e. keep the goods) but claim damages. The implied terms regarding goods being free from third parties' rights are classified as "warranties", where a breach is relatively less serious but could give rise to a claim for damages. The current legislation also sets out statutory remedies for consumers, where the implied terms regarding quality, fitness for purpose and corresponding to descriptions or samples are breached in contracts other than for hire or hire purchase. The statutory remedies are repair or replacement of goods, followed in some circumstances by termination of contract or receiving an appropriate reduction from the price.

44. In 2008 the Law Commission and Scottish Law Commission consulted on "Consumer Remedies for Faulty Goods", and published a report in 2009. Some of the provisions in this Chapter build on the Law Commissions' recommendations.

45. In 2010 the Department for Business, Innovation and Skills ("BIS") commissioned a report, entitled "Consolidation and Simplification of UK Consumer Law"[19] to examine how existing consumer law might be consolidated and simplified to make it more accessible to consumers, business and their advisers. That report recommended that consumer contract law would be improved if many of the provisions could be brought together into a single consumer contract law that so far as possible subjected all consumer supply contracts to the same rights and remedies. The report recommended that the remedies for goods would be made clearer and more accessible by incorporating them into a single piece of legislation and aligning the remedies as much as possible.

46. Following these reports, BIS consulted in July 2012 on proposals for reform of the law regarding contractual supplies to consumers of goods, as well as of services and digital content. This consultation included proposals building on the 2009 and 2010 reports.

47. A draft Bill was published in June 2013[20] and scrutinised by the House of Commons Business Innovation and Skills Committee. The Committee published its report in December 2013[21].

What goods contracts are covered?

Sections 3-8: Consumer contracts about goods

48. Section 3 sets out what contracts are covered by Chapter 2. The provisions contained in this Chapter apply in most cases where a trader agrees to supply goods to a consumer under a contract – such a contract is referred to in the Act as a "contract to supply goods". Chapter 2 applies whether the goods are supplied immediately or the parties agree that the trader will supply them at a future time. (The terms "trader", "consumer" and "goods" are addressed in section 2).

49. *Subsection* (3) provides that the Chapter does not apply to certain contracts. Such contracts therefore do not count as "contracts to supply goods".

50. Subsection (3)(a) of section 3 excludes from scope contracts where the goods in question are coins or notes to be used for currency, though coins and notes supplied for another purpose (e.g. bought as a collector's item) are covered.

51. Subsection (3)(b) of section 3 excludes items sold by execution or authority of law. This reflects the CRD and the CSD and excludes from the definition of goods items sold in situations such as a sale by an official under a legal authority to satisfy a debt (e.g. an official authorised to sell off property of a bankrupt).

52. Subsection (3)(d) of section 3 serves to prevent a contract from counting as a contract to supply goods and thus the protections under the Act from applying if the agreement is not supported by consideration other than being executed as a deed (as under the law of England and Wales and of Northern Ireland, a contract lacking consideration will only be enforceable if it is made as a deed, a written document whose signature involves certain limited formalities). The meaning of "consideration" is set out in paragraph 31. This subsection does not apply to Scotland. Subsection (3)(e) applies in relation to Scotland, as contracts may be gratuitous under Scottish law, which does not require consideration in order to form a contract. The provisions of this Chapter apply only where a contract is not gratuitous; that is, where both parties give something.

---

19 The report was authored by Professor Geraint Howells and Professor Christian Twigg-Flesner available at: https://www.gov.uk/government/uploads/system/uploads/attachment_data/file/31838/10-1255-consolidation-simplification-uk-consumer-law.pdf

20 Draft Consumer Rights Bill (URN: BIS/13/925)

21 Draft Consumer Rights Bill; sixth report of session 2013-2014

53. Under *subsection* (5), contracts to supply goods also fall within the scope of this Chapter if they involve the transfer of a share in the goods, whether between current owners or if one owner transfers their share to a third party.

54. Whilst this Chapter applies to contracts for the supply of goods, there is some variation in how particular provisions apply according to the contract type (for example some of the provisions apply in a different way to hire contracts as the consumer is not paying for ownership of the goods, but for use of them). *Subsection* (6) indicates that more specific provisions for the particular contract types take precedence.

55. *Subsection* (7) provides that with regard to any of the specific types of contracts defined in the following sections, the provisions apply whether goods are supplied alone or alongside a service and/or digital content.

56. Section 4 defines "ownership of goods" as referred to in Chapter 2 as being the general property in goods, which is the right over goods which an absolute owner has. It can be contrasted with more limited "special property" in a thing, which means that the person with special property can only put the item to a particular use rather than having absolute rights of ownership. The general rule is that ownership of the goods transfers to the consumer when the parties intend it to do so. The intention to transfer the ownership of the goods from the trader to the consumer will be dependent on the terms of the contract, what has been decided between the trader and the consumer and the circumstances of the case. The definition of "ownership of goods" is consistent with the meaning of "property" in goods under the SGA.

57. Section 18 of the SGA sets out the rules (for contracts of sale, to which the SGA applies) for ascertaining intention as to the time that ownership transfers, unless a different intention appears from the contract or circumstances. Section 4 points to this and other specific provisions in the SGA (sections 16 to 19, 20A and 20B) about the passing of property, which will apply for determining when ownership of goods is transferred under a contract of sale of goods (that is, a contract to which SGA applies).

58. Sections 5 to 8 define the types of contract to supply goods to which particular provisions apply, or apply differently.

- Section 5 defines "sales contracts". This is consistent with the category of "sales contract" under the CRD and certain provisions of this Chapter which derive from the CRD therefore apply to this category of contracts. For a contract to supply goods to be a sales contract, the goods must have a monetary price. The strict legal position may be that a contract where the trader agrees to accept something other than cash, i.e. loyalty points, could be a sales contract but under the Act sales contracts and contracts for the transfer of goods both attract the same rights under sections 9-18 and remedies under sections 19-24. Under section 3(7) the category of "sales contracts" includes contracts under which services or digital content are provided as well as the contract being for transfer of goods.

- *Subsection* (2) of section 5 clarifies that a contract where the trader agrees to manufacture or produce the goods is a sales contract. For example, where a tailor produces a made-to-measure suit for a consumer, the contract between tailor and consumer would still be a sales contract for the finished suit.

- *Subsection* (3) of section 5 clarifies that the category of sales contract includes conditional sales contracts where goods are paid for in instalments and the trader retains ownership of the goods until the conditions in the contract have been met, whether the consumer has possession of the goods in the meantime or not.

- Section 6 defines contracts for the hire of goods, as they apply between a trader and a consumer. The meaning of this provision is consistent with the definitions under sections 6 and 11G of the SGSA (save that it applies only to trader to consumer contracts, as does all of this Part of the Act), but the opportunity is being taken to simplify the wording. A contract for the hire of goods is covered by the Act irrespective of the consideration given by the consumer i.e. whether the consumer pays cash or exchanges goods in return (provided that the contract falls within section 3).

- Section 7 defines hire-purchase agreements for goods, as they apply between a trader and a consumer. This is consistent with the definitions in section 189 of the Consumer Credit Act 1974 and section 15 of the SGITA, save that it applies only to trader to consumer contracts (as does all of this Part of the Act).
- Section 8 defines contracts for transfer of goods by a trader to a consumer which are not sales contracts or hire-purchase agreements. A contract would be a contract for transfer rather than a sales contract if either (i) there is no monetary value assigned, or (ii) the contract is a mixed contract whether for a monetary price or not and, whilst goods are supplied, the transfer of goods is not sufficiently central to the contract to be a sales contract. If no monetary value is assigned to the goods, this does not preclude money from forming part of the consideration of the contract. For example, if the trader offers goods A in exchange for goods B and a cash fee, no value has been assigned to either goods A or B so the contract would fall under section 8, despite some money changing hands. The statutory rights under chapter 2 (see sections 9-18) are the same for sales contracts and contracts for transfer.

What statutory rights are there under a goods contract?

59. Sections 9 to 17 set out requirements which the goods supplied, or the trader, must meet. Under sections 9 to 14 and 17, the contracts are to be treated as containing terms that the relevant requirements will be met - or, in the case of section 12, certain details are to be treated as a term of the contract. That is to say that the requirements set by these provisions form part of the contract without either party needing to refer to them.

60. Sections 9 to 11 and 13 to 15 re-transpose Article 2 of the CSD, regarding conformity of goods with the contract. The original transposition was made in the Sale and Supply of Goods to Consumers Regulations 2002 (SI 2002/3045) which amended the SGA and the SGSA. (A transposition note setting out how the main elements of this Directive are transposed in the Act is annexed to these explanatory notes – please see Annex B).

Section 9: Goods to be of satisfactory quality

61. This section provides that goods supplied under a contract to supply goods (as defined in section 3 above) must be of satisfactory quality. It details aspects of quality which may be considered when assessing whether the goods are satisfactory – although the section only gives an indication of such aspects, not an exhaustive list. This section corresponds to section 14 SGA, section 10 SGITA and sections 4, 9, 11D and 11J SGSA in so far as they relate to satisfactory quality. But as with all of this Part it only relates to trader to consumer contracts.

62. *Subsection* (2) provides that the test of whether or not the quality of the goods is satisfactory is determined by what a reasonable person would consider satisfactory for the goods in question, taking into consideration all relevant circumstances including any description, the price and any public statements by the trader or producer or their representatives, such as statements made in advertisements or on the labels of goods. For example, a lower standard might be expected of cheap or disposable goods in comparison to an equivalent item that cost more or was advertised as being particularly durable.

63. *Subsections* (5) and (6) provide that the circumstances to be considered include public statements about the goods, for example, any claims made in advertising or labelling. However, under *subsection* (7) such statements are not to be considered as relevant if the trader was not (and could not reasonably have been expected to be) aware of the statement or if the statement was withdrawn or corrected before the contract was made.

The statement is also not to be considered if the consumer's decision could not have been influenced by it.

64. *Subsection* (4) provides that if the consumer is made aware of a particular defect before making the contract then that defect will not be grounds for finding the goods to be unsatisfactory. If the consumer examined the goods before making the contract then a defect which should have been revealed by the examination will not be grounds for finding the goods to be unsatisfactory. If the goods were supplied by sample (even if the consumer did not actually examine the sample) then a defect which should have been revealed by a reasonable examination of the sample will not be grounds for finding the goods to be unsatisfactory.

Section 10: Goods to be fit for particular purpose

65. This section provides that if a consumer acquires goods for a specific purpose, and has made this purpose known to the trader beforehand, the goods must be fit for that purpose unless the consumer does not rely - or it would be unreasonable for the consumer to rely - on the skill or judgement of the trader. This section corresponds to section 14(3) SGA, section 10(3) SGITA and sections 4(4)-(6), 9(4)-(6), 11D(5)-(7) and 11J(5)-(7) SGSA, but as with all of this Part it only relates to trader to consumer contracts.

66. *Subsection* (2) makes similar provision for transactions in which the consumer makes the purpose known to a credit broker but actually contracts with another party. For example, a consumer buying goods in a store on a payment plan may make a contract with a finance company (which would be the trader) which is introduced by the store (as credit-broker), with the store selling the goods to the finance company in order for it to sell them to the consumer. In this situation, if the consumer makes the specific purpose known to the salesperson in the store (the credit-broker) that is sufficient and the goods must be fit for that purpose - there is no need for the consumer to also have made it known to the credit provider. "Credit-broker" is defined in section 59.

Section 11: Goods to be as described

67. This section provides that where goods are supplied by description, the goods must be as described. Goods can be supplied by description even if they are available for the consumer to see and select, for example on the shelves of a shop. This section corresponds to section 13 SGA, section 9 SGITA and sections 3, 8, 11C and 11I SGSA, but as with all of this Part it only relates to trader to consumer contracts.

68. This section also, through *subsections* (4) and (5), provides that certain information required by the Consumer Contracts (Information, Cancellation and Additional Charges) Regulations 2013 ("the 2013 Regulations"), which implement the CRD, forms part of the contract. These regulations require traders to provide certain information to consumers before consumers are bound by a contract. The information required by paragraph (a) of Schedule 1 or 2 of these regulations relates to the main characteristics of the goods. The section establishes that any information that is provided by the trader and that is about the main characteristics – so is of a category mentioned in paragraph (a) of Schedule 1 or 2 of the 2013 Regulations - forms part of the contract. If the information regarding the main characteristics is not complied with, the consumer can pursue the protections for breach of section 11, as set out in section 19.

69. Subsection (5) makes clear that any change made to this information before entering into the contract or at a later date will not be effective on the contract unless agreed by both the trader and the consumer (although it may not be necessary to do so where the pre-contract information itself reflects the fact that the particular potential changes envisaged may be made). Nor can the parties agree a change which would deprive the consumer of his or her rights under this Chapter (see section 31).

70. *Subsection* (6) makes clear that the provisions of subsections (4) and (5) apply to a contract for sale of second hand goods which are sold at a public auction, if individuals

can attend the auction sale in person. Most of the provisions of Chapter 2 do not apply in these circumstances, as explained further in relation to section 2(5).

Section 12: Other pre-contract information included in contract

71. This section establishes that any other information provided by the trader which is of a category mentioned in Schedule 1 or 2 of the 2013 Regulations, but which does not relate to main characteristics of the goods so does not fall under section 11, also forms part of the contract between the trader and the consumer. If this information is not accurate then the consumer may recover some money – see section 19(5) - but the other remedies (right to reject, repair, replacement etc) are not available.

72. *Subsection* (3) makes clear that the trader will not however be able to change this information without the consumer's agreement (although it may not be necessary to do so where the pre-contract information itself reflects the fact that the particular potential changes envisaged may be made), so there would be a breach of contract if the information provided was not correct when the contract was made. Nor can the parties agree a change which would deprive the consumer of his or her rights under this Chapter (see section 31).

73. *Subsection* (4) makes clear that the provisions of this section apply to a contract for sale of second hand goods which are sold at a public auction, if individuals can attend the auction sale in person. Most of the provisions of Chapter 2 do not apply in these circumstances, as explained further in relation to section 2(5).

Section 13: Goods to match a sample

74. Under this section, if a consumer enters into a contract for goods on the basis of a sample, the final goods delivered must match the sample, except that any differences brought to the consumer's attention before the contract is made would not breach this requirement. This differs from the following section (Goods to match a model seen or examined) in that a sample is usually only a representative part of the whole goods in question. An example is a consumer buying curtains after having looked at a swatch of the material. This section replaces section 15 SGA, section 11 SGITA and sections 5, 10, 11E and 11K SGSA for trader to consumer contracts.

75. Where goods are held out as a sample then section 13 will be breached if the full goods supplied do not match that sample or they have a defect which makes their quality unsatisfactory (under section 9) and which the consumer would not have discovered by a reasonable examination of the sample goods.

Section 14: Goods to match a model seen or examined

76. This section establishes that if the trader displays or provides a model of the goods in question, then the goods received should match that model, except that any differences brought to the consumer's attention before the contract is made would not breach this protection.

77. An example is a consumer viewing a television on the shop floor but receiving a boxed television from the stockroom. Under this section the delivered model should match the viewed model (unless any differences are brought to the consumer's attention before it is bought).

Section 15: Installation as part of conformity of the goods with the contract

78. Section 15 makes clear that special rules apply where goods are both supplied and installed by a trader (or the installation is done under that same trader's responsibility). In that case, if the installation service is done incorrectly then the goods remedies apply, with the exception of the short-term right to reject.

Section 16: Goods not conforming to contract if digital content does not conform

79. Section 16 makes clear that special rules also apply where goods and digital content are supplied together in one product (e.g. where digital content is supplied on a disk). In that case, section 16 makes clear that if the digital content rights are not met then this will mean the goods are substandard and the consumer has the right to the full suite of goods remedies (including the short-term right to reject).

Section 17: Trader to have right to supply the goods etc

80. This section protects the consumer by making it a term of the contract that the trader has the right to sell or transfer the goods or to transfer possession of them, at the point when the transfer of ownership or possession takes place. In some transactions, the sale, transfer or hire will be immediate so the trader will need to have this right at the time the contract is made. In other cases, the parties may agree that the goods will be sold, transferred or hired at a later stage – the trader must have this right at that later time. This section corresponds to section 12 SGA, section 8 SGITA and sections 2, 7, 11B and 11H SGSA. But as with all of this Part it only relates to trader to consumer contracts. The general rule is that ownership transfers when the parties intend it to transfer. For contracts of sale (that is, contracts to which SGA applies), rules on establishing the parties' intention as to the time ownership transfers - unless a different intention arises from the contract or the circumstances - are found in SGA, in particular section 18 (note, however, that legislation refers to "property" as opposed to "ownership" though the meaning is the same). See the notes on section 4 for further information.

81. The section also guarantees that no other person should have rights over the goods (e.g. a right to use the goods) unless the consumer is made aware of this before making the contract and that the consumer's possession of the goods should not be disturbed by anyone with rights over the goods (except any rights of which the consumer is made aware). These protections do not apply to hire contracts.

82. In the case of hire contracts, there will be other parties with rights over the goods – for example, the goods will be owned by someone other than the consumer, as the consumer is not contracting to own the goods but only to use them. Under *subsection* (3), the consumer's use of the goods may only be interrupted by the owner of the goods or by any third party with rights over the goods if the consumer has been informed of that person's rights over the goods before making the contract.

83. This section does not affect the protection for private purchasers of motor vehicles under section 27 Hire-Purchase Act 1964. Under that provision, where a private purchaser buys a motor vehicle from someone who has it subject to a hire-purchase agreement or conditional sale agreement and does not yet properly own the vehicle (because it is still under the hire-purchase or conditional sale agreement), then, if the private purchaser is a purchaser in good faith and without notice of the hire-purchase agreement or conditional sale agreement, the transaction is treated as if the person selling the vehicle did properly own it.

Section 18: No other requirement to treat term about quality or fitness as included

84. This section corresponds to section 14(1) of the SGA, but for contracts between a trader and consumer. The section serves to state that, unless there is an express term concerning the quality of the goods or the goods' fitness for a particular purpose, or a term implied by another enactment, the contract should not be treated as including any such terms, other than those set out in sections 9, 10, 13 and (where it applies) 16.

What remedies are there if statutory rights under a goods contract are not met?

85. Sections 19 to 24 set out the remedies that apply if the consumer's statutory rights covered in sections 9 to 17 are not met.

86. Sections 19 and 23 to 24 re-transpose Article 3 of the CSD (originally transposed by the Sale and Supply of Goods to Consumers Regulations 2002 which amended the SGA and the SGSA). (A transposition note setting out how the main elements of this Directive are transposed in the Act is annexed to these explanatory notes – please see Annex B).

Section 19: Consumer's rights to enforce terms about goods

87. Depending on the statutory right which is breached, the consumer may have a short-term right to reject, a right to have the goods repaired or replaced and/or (if this is not possible or fails to address the fault) a right to have the purchase price reduced (and keep the goods) or a final right to reject the goods, or a right to recover certain costs. *Subsections* (1) and (3) to (6) outline these rights and also serve to signpost the reader to the relevant sections that detail these remedies and their application.

88. *Subsection* (2) makes clear that if a statutory right is breached due to the goods not conforming to the relevant term (e.g. to be of satisfactory quality), if the non-conformity is due to the materials supplied by the consumer, then this does not count as a failure to conform to the contract.

89. *Subsection* (5) makes clear that if the trader is in breach of any pre-contract information required to be treated as part of the contract by section 12, the consumer has the right to recover any costs which they incurred as a result of the breach. The consumer can recover the amount of these costs up to the full price of the goods (so they could receive a full refund), or the full amount they already paid (if they had only paid in part for the goods). This applies equally where there is other consideration given instead of a price – the cap on the recoverable costs would be the value of that consideration. If the consumer incurs costs or losses above this amount, they may be able to seek damages for breach of contract (see *subsection* (9)).

90. Under subsection (6), if the requirement for the trader to have the right to sell or transfer the goods or possession of them (section 17(1)) is breached, the consumer has a right to reject the goods, as described further in section 20. The right to reject in this instance is not a short-term right to reject nor a final right to reject, therefore section 22 and section 24 respectively do not apply. The other rights provided by section 17 – that no other person should have rights over the goods, unless the consumer is made aware of this before making the contract and that the consumer's possession of the goods should not be disturbed by anyone with rights over the goods – are covered by subsections (9) and (10), as breach of these rights does not give rise to a right to reject or the other statutory remedies, but the consumer may seek damages.

91. *Subsection* (7) makes clear that the availability of remedies specified in subsections (3) to (6) is subject to the particular rules for delivery of the wrong quantity and instalment deliveries in sections 25 and 26. If a trader delivers the wrong quantity of goods then the remedies will be determined by section 25. If the parties agree that the goods will be delivered in instalments, any entitlement to exercise the short-term right to reject or the right to reject under section 19(6) will be determined in accordance with section 26.

92. *Subsection* (8) states that the remedies for a breach of a term in the contract about the time or period for the delivery of goods are set out in section 28.

93. Subsections (9) and (10) serve as a reminder that the statutory remedies set out in section 19 do not mean the consumer cannot pursue other remedies, as an alternative or addition to the statutory remedies but the consumer may not recover more than once for the same loss. For example, in some cases the consumer may exercise the short-term right to reject and receive a refund, and also claim damages for additional loss caused by the non-conformity of the goods. In other cases, a consumer may prefer to claim damages instead of pursuing one of the statutory remedies.

94. *Subsection* (11) outlines the other common law remedies that the consumer may be able to seek, such as claiming damages or relying on the breach to relieve the consumer of

the obligation to pay the price or some of it (essentially setting the breach off against the price), and that the consumer may pursue equitable remedies. For a breach of an express term (that is a term which the parties expressly agree to) the consumer may be able to treat the contract as at an end, depending on the status of that term. For example, if the consumer and the trader agree an express term in the contract that is so important that a subsequent breach of that term by the trader would leave the consumer deprived of substantially the whole benefit that was intended from the contract, the consumer could treat the contract as at an end.

95. *Subsection* (12) provides that the consumer is only entitled to treat the contract as at an end for breach of one of the statutory rights in sections 9-11, 13-16 or 17(1) by exercising a right to reject under Chapter 2. This overrides any common law right to terminate the contract for breach of the terms which these sections require to be treated as included in the contract.

96. *Subsection* (13) clarifies that references in Part 1 to treating a contract as "at an end" have the same meaning as treating a contract as "repudiated". This means that, where a consumer treats a goods contract as at an end under the Act, the consumer may also be able to recover damages for non-performance of the whole contract by the trader.

97. *Subsections* (14) and (15) provide that, if a breach of the statutory rights – for example a fault - arises in the first 6 months from delivery, it is presumed to have been present at the time of delivery unless the trader proves otherwise or this presumption is incompatible with the nature of the goods or the particular breach or fault. This applies where the consumer exercises their right to a repair or replacement or their right to a price reduction or the final right to reject. This does not apply where the consumer exercises the short-term right to reject. These subsections correspond to section 48A(3) and (4) of the SGA and section 11M(3) and (4) of the SGSA.

98. For goods, sections 19 and 20 provide that in certain situations the consumer has the right to terminate the contract and receive a refund. Where the contract is a mixed contract with a goods element, this means (unless the contract is severable, see paragraph 100 below) that the consumer has the right to terminate the whole contract (both the goods and non-goods elements) and receive a refund of the price of the contract (or for money already paid towards the full price of the contract). If the consumer wishes to continue part of the contract, it is open to the parties to agree to do so.

99. For example, a consumer contracts with a trader to source for them and then install a kitchen. When the trader has finished the work, the granite worktops (the goods) are badly scratched and not fit for purpose. The consumer may ask for their money back, that is any money paid for both the installation service and the kitchen units.

100. As a further example, a consumer purchases a mobile phone handset (goods) with a network service contract. The phone keeps crashing so they return it to the trader. The consumer has the right to ask for a refund for both the phone and service, however in practice they may want to continue with the service to use with another phone, and the consumer and trader could agree to that. The consumer's right to terminate a whole contract (as explained in paragraph 98) is subject to the rules on severable contracts which are explained in paragraphs 119 to 121 below (and in paragraph 124 where partial rejection is concerned).

101. In summary, the statutory remedies that potentially apply for breach of the consumer's statutory rights are as follows:

Statutory right being breached	***Statutory remedies that may apply***
Goods to be of satisfactory quality (section 9)	• The short-term right to reject (sections 20-22) • The right to repair or replacement (section 23)

Statutory right being breached	***Statutory remedies that may apply***
	• The right to a price reduction or the final right to reject (section 24)
Goods to be fit for particular purpose (section 10)	• The short-term right to reject (sections 20-22) • The right to repair or replacement (section 23) • The right to a price reduction or the final right to reject (section 24)
Goods to be as described (section 11), including conforming to information re material characteristics under the CRD	• The short-term right to reject (sections 20-22) • The right to repair or replacement (section 23) • The right to a price reduction or the final right to reject (section 24)
Conformity with contract information provided pursuant to the 2013 Regulations (section 12)	• The right to recover costs incurred, up to the contract price (section 19(5))
Goods to match a sample (section 13)	• The short-term right to reject (sections 20-22) • The right to repair or replacement (section 23) • The right to a price reduction or the final right to reject (section 24)
Goods to match a model seen or examined (section 14)	• The short-term right to reject (sections 20-22) • The right to repair or replacement (section 23) • The right to a price reduction or the final right to reject (section 24)
Incorrect installation of goods (by trader or under trader's responsibility) (section 15)	• The right to repair or replacement (section 23) • The right to a price reduction or the final right to reject (section 24)
Goods not conforming to contract if digital content does not conform (section 16)	• The short-term right to reject (sections 20-22) • The right to repair or replacement (section 23) • The right to a price reduction or the final right to reject (section 24)
Trader to have right to sell or transfer the goods or to transfer possession (section 17(1))	• The right to reject (section 20)
Goods to be free from any charge or encumbrance not disclosed or known (section 17 (2) and (5))	• Statutory remedies do not apply but consumers may claim damages (section 19(9) and (10))
Consumer to enjoy quiet possession of the goods (section 17(2), (3), (6) and (7))	• Statutory remedies do not apply but consumers may claim damages (section 19(9) and (10))

102. As set out above, the terms that are to be treated as included in the contract in sections 9-17 are contractual terms and if they are not met it means there is a breach of contract. The common law (that is, law that is set out in cases decided by judges) already provides certain remedies for breach of contract. Subsections (9) to (11) of section 19 serve as a reminder that the consumer may – instead of (or, in some cases, in addition to) pursuing the statutory remedies set out in section 19 and subsequent sections – seek common law or other (equitable) remedies. These may include damages, specific performance or (in Scotland) specific implement, or a right to treat the contract as terminated for breach of an express term in some cases (see also paragraph 94).

103. "Damages" refers to the common law remedy of financial compensation paid by one party to the other. For example, where a trader is in breach of a term that this Part requires to be treated as included in a contract, the court may order the trader to pay damages to the consumer. Generally, an award of damages for breach of contract is intended to compensate the injured party for loss suffered. In some, less frequent, cases the court may award damages which go beyond simply compensating the consumer for loss suffered – e.g. a court can sometimes award nominal damages, where there is a breach of contract but no loss, or aggravated damages to compensate for mental distress. For a breach of a term that this Part requires to be treated as included in the contract, the general rule is that damages are intended to put the consumer in the same position as if there had not been a breach. The level of damages awarded will depend on the specific circumstances and the term which the trader has breached. Typically, damages would cover the estimated loss directly resulting from the breach, in the ordinary course of events: if the consumer keeps the goods, this would generally be the difference between the value of the goods, service or digital content received by the consumer and the value had there not been a breach. Damages may cover loss or damage caused by the faulty goods, for example, where a faulty washing machine damages clothing while in use. There are legal tests to be satisfied for a consumer to recover damages: a person can only recover damages for loss which was caused by the breach (of the term required by the Act) and which was sufficiently foreseeable; and the consumer cannot recover for loss which they could reasonably have acted to limit or mitigate.

104. "Specific performance" is a direction a court can make, to compel a party to perform their obligations under a contract. It is an equitable remedy, meaning it is not available to consumers as a right, but at the court's discretion. It will not be ordered if damages (see above) are adequate to compensate the consumer – generally, damages will be adequate unless the subject matter of the contract is unique, as the consumer can use damages to buy a replacement. "Specific implement" is similar to "specific performance" for Scotland, and there are likewise specific circumstances where that may be used. In referring to specific performance or specific implement, this section does not seek to codify the law as to when specific performance or specific implement might be available, but the references serve as a reminder that it may be an alternative remedy to the statutory remedies. Section 58 gives more detail on the powers of the court in proceedings where a remedy is sought.

105. Under the law of England and Wales and of Northern Ireland, claims for breach of contract are subject to a limitation period of six years from the date of the breach of contract, whereas in Scottish law the limitation period is five years. Because the protections provided under this Part of the Act operate on the basis of contract law, the consumer has 6 years (or 5 years in Scotland) within which they may pursue remedies for breach of one of the statutory rights. This does not mean that a consumer may seek a remedy under the Act for any fault arising in goods at any time in the six (or five) years following delivery, but only if one of the statutory rights is breached. The statutory right under section 9 (goods to be of satisfactory quality) will only be breached if goods are not of the standard which a reasonable person would consider to be satisfactory, taking into account circumstances including the price and any description given. This test of reasonableness is provided under section 9(2). For example, the statutory right may not be breached and so a consumer would not be able to obtain a remedy if, say, a very cheap kettle stopped working fully after four years, as a reasonable person might not expect a bottom of the range kettle to last that long.

Section 20: ***Right to reject***

106. This section serves to explain the remedies of short-term right to reject, final right to reject and the right to reject under section 19(6), and how these operate.

107. The section establishes that when the consumer has one of these rights to reject and chooses to exercise it, this means rejecting the goods and terminating the contract. The section also provides what the consumer must do to exercise the right.

108. *Subsection* (5) sets out what the consumer must do to exercise one of these rights: they must indicate to the trader that they are rejecting the goods and treating the contract as at an end.

109. *Subsection* (6) clarifies that, as long as the meaning of the indication is clear, it does not matter what form it takes.

110. *Subsection* (7) provides that when the right to reject is exercised by the consumer, the trader has a duty to refund the consumer and from this time the consumer must make the goods available for collection by the trader, or if agreed, return the rejected goods to the trader.

111. *Subsection* (8) clarifies that any reasonable costs of returning rejected goods to the trader (except where the consumer returns the goods in person to where they obtained physical possession of them) is to be borne by the trader. This includes the trader paying postal costs. This applies whether or not the consumer has agreed to return the goods, as mentioned in subsection (7).

112. Subsection (8) does not prevent a consumer from pursuing a damages claim. For example, a consumer might wish to do so in circumstances where returning the goods to the place that the consumer obtained physical possession of them does incur quite substantial costs for the consumer.

113. *Subsection* (10) provides that where a refund is to be provided and the original payment (or part of it) was made with money, the consumer is entitled to money back for the money they paid, so the trader may not substitute store vouchers, credit or an equivalent in place of the required monetary refund.

114. If money was not used to pay for the goods, under *subsections* (11) and (12), the consumer is not entitled to money back but the "refund" would be a return of whatever the consumer gave in exchange for the goods (see examples below). If this cannot be returned to the consumer due to the nature of the exchange, then, under *subsection* (18) and (19), the consumer may not demand a refund but may pursue a damages claim. The consumer still has a "right to reject" (that is, to reject the goods and treat the contract as at an end) in this situation, but the means of obtaining money back is different. Examples of situations where these subsections may apply include:

- A toy "bought" with vouchers collected from cereal packets. In this case it would be possible to return equivalent vouchers (even though they would not necessarily be the actual vouchers that the consumer cut out) and a "refund" could therefore take that form under subsection (11).
- A microwave supplied to the consumer by a trader specialising in refurbishment of white-goods, in exchange for the consumer's old fridge-freezer. In this case, if the fridge-freezer was still available in an unchanged state, then this could be returned to the consumer as a "refund" under subsection (12), but if it was no longer available, or had been refurbished, then a refund would not be possible.

115. Where money formed part of what the consumer used to pay for the goods but the rest was "paid for" with something else (something non-monetary), the consumer is still entitled to a refund for the money that they paid and return of the other property transferred if possible. The consumer may pursue a damages claim for any loss for which they cannot claim a "refund" (of money or property) under section 20.

116. *Subsection* (13) provides that, in the specific case of hired goods, the consumer may not claim a refund on any money paid (or whatever was transferred in place of money) for hire that the consumer enjoyed. Any refund will only cover money paid for a period of hire that was lost due to the contract being ended. For example, if a consumer hired goods for 1 month and paid in advance, but after 3 weeks a fault manifested so the consumer exercised their short-term right to reject, the consumer would only be able to seek a refund for the remaining 1 week when the goods would not be used. The

consumer may also have a claim in damages to compensate them for some of the hire charges paid during the period in which the consumer had the faulty goods but before they rejected them. Under *subsection* (18)(c), if something other than money was transferred in exchange for the hire of the goods, and this cannot be divided to account for the time that the consumer has not had use of the goods, no refund may be pursued. The consumer could instead claim damages. If what the consumer transferred can be divided but not into the portion to which the consumer would be entitled under subsection (13), a refund of the division can be pursued, even if this is less than the proportional amount transferred by the consumer for the period of use of the goods. The consumer could then claim damages for the remainder.

117. *Subsection* (14) establishes that for contracts other than hire, and where payments for the goods are made over time (conditional sale and hire purchase contracts), any claim for a refund can only be made against money that has already been paid up to that point. For example if a £500 washing machine was found to be faulty after the consumer had paid £350, the maximum refund would be £350.

118. *Subsection* (15) requires a trader to provide any refund due to the consumer without undue delay and at the latest within 14 days from when the trader agrees that the consumer is entitled to it. For example, if a consumer rejects goods because of a technical fault which cannot be seen without testing or detailed examination, the 14-day period would start once the trader had carried out the appropriate tests and found the goods were indeed faulty. In contrast, if it was clear from looking at the goods that they breached the relevant requirement under the Act, there is unlikely to be any reason for the trader not to agree immediately that the consumer is entitled to a refund. In any case, there must be no undue delay, so the trader could not delay payment unnecessarily, for example in order to wait for time-consuming tests which are completely irrelevant. *Subsection* (16) provides that, where the consumer paid money under the contract, the refund must be given in the same form as the original payment unless the consumer agrees otherwise. For example, a consumer who paid cash should receive cash rather than, say, a cheque unless they agree to this. Under *subsection* (17), no fee may be charged for the provision of a refund.

119. *Subsections* (20) and (21) clarify how rejection of goods works where a contract is severable. That is where the contract was intended to be divisible, so different parts of the consideration can be assigned to different parts of the performance – e.g. an agreement to pay pro-rata for some goods supplied, no matter whether others are supplied.

120. Where a contract is severable, if the fault is with goods in one part of the contract, the consumer has a right to reject those goods and effectively terminate that part of the contract. Beyond that it is a question of the circumstances as to whether the consumer may or may not reject other goods and effectively terminate the whole of the contract.

121. Subsections (20) and (21) do not apply in relation to Scotland.

Section 21: Partial rejection of goods

122. This section clarifies the consumer's rights around partial rejection of goods. If the consumer has the right to reject the goods because some or all of them do not conform to the contract then the consumer can reject some or all of them. If the consumer rejects only some of the goods they cannot reject any of the goods which do conform to the contract. That is, the consumer can:

- reject all of the goods (conforming and non-conforming);
- reject all of the non-conforming goods (but none of the conforming goods); or
- reject some of the non-conforming goods (and keep some of the non-conforming goods and all of the conforming goods).

123. If the consumer has the right to reject an instalment of goods because some or all of them do not conform to the contract, then the consumer can reject some or all of the goods in the instalment. If the consumer rejects some of the goods they cannot reject any of the goods in the instalment which do conform to the contract.

124. If the contract is severable and the consumer has the right to reject goods supplied under one part of the contract because they do not conform to the contract, then the consumer can reject some or all of those goods. If the consumer chooses to reject only some of the goods they are entitled to reject, they cannot reject any of those goods which do conform to the contract.

125. In this section, conforming to the contract means conforming to any of the requirements of the contract. This includes conforming to all of the terms which the Act requires to be treated as included in a contract to supply goods, including under section 17. In this way, conforming to the contract has a wider meaning than in sections 19 and 22-24, which do not cover conformity to the terms required by section 17.

126. The provision is in effect consistent with section 35A of SGA, although section 35A provides that acceptance of some goods does not prevent rejection of others, whereas that concept of acceptance does not apply under the Act. This section therefore provides clarity that the consumer nonetheless has equivalent rights to reject in part.

127. *Subsections* (3) and (4) correspond to section 35(7) of the SGA and provide that where the goods form part of a "commercial unit" (defined in subsection (4)) the consumer may not reject some of the goods in that unit but keep others. For example, if furniture was sold as a three-piece-suite, but there was a fault with one of the chairs, the consumer would not be entitled to reject only the chair.

*Section 22: **Time limit for short-term right to reject***

128. This section establishes the minimum time limit of 30 days for the short-term right to reject. The one exception (established under *subsection* (4)) is that for perishable goods which would not be reasonably expected to last longer than 30 days, the period for exercising the short-term right to reject lasts only as long as it would be reasonable to expect those goods to last.

129. The 30 day period begins the day after the latest of the following:

- The consumer obtains ownership of the goods (i.e. the consumer buys the goods) or, for hire, hire-purchase or conditional sales, obtains possession.
- The goods have been delivered.
- If applicable, the trader has notified the consumer that any actions required before the goods may be used (including installation, if needed) have been completed by the trader.

130. This section also provides that the 30 day period will not run during any repair or replacement (the waiting period). On return of the goods to the consumer, the consumer has the remainder of the 30-day period, or 7 days (whichever is longer), within which they can still exercise the short-term right to reject if the goods still breach the standards set by the Act.

131. *Subsection* (8) details when the waiting period starts and ends. The period starts on the day the consumer requests the repair or replacement and ends on the day that the consumer receives the repaired or replacement goods.

*Section 23: **Right to repair or replacement***

132. This section details a consumer's right to insist on repair or replacement of faulty goods, the cost of which must be borne by the trader. This includes the trader bearing any costs involved in the removal of an installed item and reinstallation of a replacement.

A replacement would usually need to be identical, that is of the same make and model and if the goods were bought new then the replacement would need to be new.

133. Once the consumer has opted for a repair or replacement of the goods, he or she may not ask for the other of these, or exercise the short-term right to reject, without first allowing the trader a reasonable time to complete that chosen remedy. However, if waiting a reasonable time would cause the consumer significant inconvenience then the consumer can pursue an alternative remedy without doing so.

Section 24: ***Right to price reduction or final right to reject***

134. This section provides for the consumer's rights to reduction of the purchase price or to reject the goods and obtain a (partial) refund. These are generally available if repair or replacement of the goods has not been possible or has not corrected the fault. Under *subsection* (4), if the consumer transferred something other than money for the goods, and the thing transferred cannot be returned in the same state or divided sufficiently to give back to the consumer the appropriate amount the consumer may not seek a reduction in the purchase price.

135. This section largely corresponds to section 48C of the SGA and section 11P of the SGSA, but there are some changes as outlined below.

136. The section provides that, if repair or replacement was impossible or if the consumer's goods continue to be substandard after the consumer has either:

- already undergone one repair or replacement of the goods by the trader; or
- sought a repair or replacement but this was not carried out within a reasonable time or without significant inconvenient to the consumer,

the consumer may either:

- keep the goods and insist on a reduction in the price; or
- reject the goods and obtain a refund which may, in some circumstances, be subject to a deduction to take account of any use the consumer has had of the goods.

137. For the purposes of determining when one repair has been carried out, *subsection* (7) provides that, where the repair is carried out on the consumer's premises, the repair is not complete until the trader indicates to the consumer that the repairs are finished. This means that a single repair may be carried out over more than one visit, without triggering the right to a price reduction or the final right to reject until the trader notifies the consumer that it is complete.

138. Where the consumer requests that a number of faults be repaired, and these repairs are provided together, this counts as a single repair.

139. If the consumer opts to keep the goods and require a reduction in price the question of what is an appropriate amount will depend on the circumstances and the remaining functionality of the goods. It is intended that the reduction in price should reflect the difference in value between what the consumer paid for and the value of what they actually receive, and could be as much as a full refund or the full amount already paid.

140. Where the trader is required to provide a refund because the consumer had paid more than the reduced price, the refund must be provided to the consumer without undue delay and at the latest within 14 days from when the trader agrees that the consumer is entitled to it. Where the consumer paid money under the contract, the refund must be given in the same form as the original payment unless the consumer agrees otherwise. No fee may be charged for the provision of a refund. (See paragraph 118 for further details.)

141. *Subsections* (10) to (13) provide that if the final right to reject is exercised within 6 months of delivery of the goods (or, if later, transfer of ownership or the trader

having completed and notified the consumer of any required action), the trader must generally give the consumer a full refund. After the first 6 months, the trader may apply a deduction to the refund to account for the use that the consumer has had. There is an exception if the goods consist of a motor vehicle (as defined in *subsections* (12) and (13)). In this case a deduction for use may be made in the first 6 months. Vehicles such as mobility scooters (referred to as invalid carriages in other legislation) are excepted from the definition of motor vehicle for these purposes.

142. Subsection (10)(b) provides an order making power to extend the exemption to the 6 month rule to other types of goods. Under *subsections* (14) and (15), the power would be exercisable if the inability to apply a deduction for use to those goods in the first 6 months causes significant detriment to traders. It is subject to the affirmative resolution procedure.

Other rules about remedies under goods contracts

*Section 25: **Delivery of wrong quantity***

143. This section corresponds to section 30 of the SGA, but is not limited to sales contracts and as with all of this Part it only relates to trader to consumer contracts.

144. This section provides that the consumer may reject the goods if the wrong quantity is delivered, but if they choose to accept the goods then they must pay the contract rate for what they receive. If more is delivered than was contracted for, the consumer has the additional option to reject the excess and keep the contracted amount.

145. This section only entitles the consumer to reject goods: rules of contract law will determine whether or not the contract can be treated as at an end. This reflects the existing position under the SGA.

*Section 26: **Instalment deliveries***

146. This section corresponds substantively to section 31 of the SGA, but is not limited to sales contracts and as with all of this Part it only relates to trader to consumer contracts.

147. Under this section the consumer is not required to accept delivery in instalments unless they agree to it. If they do agree and one or more of the deliveries is defective (for example because the goods in that instalment are substandard), depending on the circumstances, the consumer may have a right to damages or to reject the goods in the relevant instalment(s), or to treat the whole contract as ended. Which of these rights applies depends on the specific circumstances and must be judged on a case-by-case basis. However, *subsection* (5) provides that, if a delivery of an instalment fails to comply with section 28, it is section 28 that applies, and not section 26.

*Section 27: **Consignation, or payment into court, in Scotland***

148. This section is based on section 58 of the SGA, but is not limited to sales contracts and as with all of this Part it only relates to trader to consumer contracts.

149. This section applies where a trader is pursuing payment from a consumer for goods that a consumer could otherwise have opted to reject but chose not to, including where the consumer argues, in answer to a demand for payment, that the price should be reduced due to the trader's breach. It provides that a Scottish court may require that consumer to pay the outstanding price (or part of it) to the court or a third party under court authority, or to provide other security. This serves to provide comfort for the trader, that the consumer will pay if the court finds that the consumer is obliged to pay the price.

Other rules about goods contracts

Section 28: Delivery of goods

150. This section implements Article 18 of the CRD and will replace regulation 42 of the 2013 Regulations. It applies only to sales contracts between traders and consumers for goods. Sales contracts are defined in section 5. If the parties have agreed that the goods are to be delivered in instalments, this section applies to delivery of each instalment. "Delivery" is defined in section 59. In addition to section 28, the rules about delivery in section 29 of SGA apply to sales contracts, with the exception of section 29(3) SGA.

151. Under this section, unless a separate agreement is reached between the consumer and trader, the trader must deliver the goods to the consumer and must do so without undue delay and within 30 days after the contract is made.

152. Where the goods are to be delivered immediately at the time the contract is made, this counts as an agreement between the parties as to the time for delivery. Therefore, if goods are not delivered immediately, the consumer is able to terminate the contract if immediate delivery was essential; otherwise, the trader may deliver again within a period specified by the consumer. It is expected that in most cases where a consumer purchases goods expecting to receive them immediately, that immediate delivery will be essential in the circumstances.

153. Where the trader refuses to deliver the goods or delivery within the initial timeframe was essential (either because the consumer told the trader that it was essential or this was implicit from the circumstances) then the consumer may treat the contract as at an end if the trader fails to meet the initial delivery period. The consumer does not have to give the trader a further opportunity to deliver in these circumstances. Examples of goods for which delivery within the initial delivery period might be taken to be essential would include a wedding dress or birthday cake.

154. In cases other than those above then, if the trader fails to deliver the goods on an agreed date or within the 30 days, under *subsection* (7), the consumer may state a further reasonable timeframe within which the trader is required to deliver the goods.

155. If the trader again fails to deliver the goods in this time frame, then the consumer may treat the contract as at an end.

156. The consumer may choose to reject some of the goods rather than treating the contract as at an end, or, where the goods have not been delivered, the consumer may cancel their order for some or all of those goods. For example, if goods are delivered after the periods required by this section, the consumer may wish to reject some of the goods but keep others, as some may no longer be of use to the consumer. If some goods are delivered on time but others are outstanding, the consumer may wish to cancel the order for some or all of the outstanding goods.

157. *Subsection (14)* makes clear that the provisions of this section apply to a contract for sale of second hand goods which are sold at a public auction, if individuals can attend the auction sale in person. Most of the provisions of Chapter 2 do not apply in these circumstances, as explained further in relation to section 2(5).

Section 29: Passing of risk

158. This section determines where risk relating to the goods supplied under a sales contract lies before and after transfer of physical possession of the goods to the consumer. Under the section, the risk lies with the trader until the consumer has physical possession of the goods, at which point risk is transferred to the consumer. However, if the consumer stipulates that the trader must use a carrier of the consumer's choosing, and that carrier was not offered by the trader as an option, the risk transfers to the consumer at the time that the goods are passed to the carrier.

159. *Subsection (6)* makes clear that the provisions of this section apply to a contract for sale of second hand goods which are sold at a public auction, if individuals can attend the auction sale in person. Most of the provisions of Chapter 2 do not apply in these circumstances, as explained further in relation to section 2(5).

Section 30: Goods offered with a guarantee

160. This section replaces regulation 15 of the Sale and Supply of Goods to Consumers Regulations 2002. These regulations transposed the CSD and regulation 15 implemented Article 6 of the CSD. This section therefore serves to transpose Article 6 again. Under this section, a guarantee provided alongside the goods without extra charge is legally binding. In particular, the guarantee must:

- be written in plain, intelligible language and, if the goods are offered in the UK, in English,
- include the name and address of the guarantor,
- state that the consumer has statutory rights (under this Act) regarding the goods which are not affected by the guarantee,
- state the duration and territorial scope of the guarantee,
- state the essential details for making claims under the guarantee, and
- be made available to the consumer in writing and within a reasonable time.

Can a trader contract out of statutory rights and remedies under a goods contract?

Section 31: Liability that cannot be excluded or restricted

161. This section serves to prevent traders from contracting out of the consumer's statutory rights under sections 9 to 16, as well as sections 28 and 29 on time of delivery and the passing of risk and, for contracts other than hire, the requirement on right to title contained in section 17. This section also has the effect that any term in a contract which seeks to prevent the consumer from having access to the statutory rights and remedies or to make exercising these rights less attractive to the consumer by either making it more difficult and onerous to do so, or by placing the consumer at a disadvantage after doing so, will also be void. For hire contracts, *subsections* (5) and (6) provide that section 31 does not prevent the parties from contracting out of the protection that the trader must have the right to transfer possession or that the consumer must enjoy quiet possession (under section 17), but a term seeking to exclude or limit these protections is subject to the test of fairness in section 62.

162. This section corresponds to sections 6 and 7 of the UCTA, but as with all of this Part it only relates to trader to consumer contracts. The section also serves to implement Article 25 of the CRD (in relation to those Articles of the CRD implemented in this Chapter) and Article 7(1) of the CSD.

163. This section also provides that an agreement to submit disputes to arbitration is not covered by this bar on excluding or restricting liability. It should be noted however that paragraph 20 of Schedule 2 makes clear that a term requiring the consumer to take disputes exclusively to arbitration may be regarded as unfair. Furthermore, the Arbitration Act 1996 provides that a term which constitutes an arbitration agreement is automatically unfair (under Part 2 of the Act, once it comes into force), if the claim is for less than an amount specified in an Order made under section 91 of the Arbitration Act. This amount is currently set at £5000 in the Unfair Arbitration Agreements (Specified Amount) Order 1999 (SI 1999/2167). It is possible that this amount may change from time to time.

Section 32: Contracts applying law of non-EEA state

164. The parties to a contract may agree that the contract is to be governed by the law of a particular country. This might be because the trader is based in a country other than the UK. The Rome I Regulation governs which laws apply to those contracts. In some circumstances, despite another law being chosen, laws of the consumer's habitual residence apply if they cannot be derogated from by agreement. See paragraph 27 for further details.

165. This section provides that most of Chapter 2 will apply to protect a consumer under a sales contract (as defined in section 5), where a contract has a close connection with the UK, even if the contract states the law of a non-EEA State applies (the EEA is the European Economic Area of the EU plus Iceland, Liechtenstein and Norway). The provision is included to comply with Article 7(2) of the CSD, which requires that the consumer should not be deprived of its protection, where a contract has a close connection with a Member State, even if the contract states the law of a non-Member State applies. It does not cover section 28 and 29, nor restriction of liability under sections 28 and 29, as these derive from the CRD which does not have this requirement.

Chapter 3 Digital Content

Summary and Background

166. Chapter 3 concerns contracts where a trader agrees to supply digital content to a consumer. "Digital content" is a key definition in Part 1 and as such is defined in section 2 (Key definitions). It is defined as data which are produced and supplied in digital form and includes software, music, computer games and applications or "apps". In the case of digital content which is supplied under contract from a trader to a consumer, and largely or wholly stored and processed remotely, such as software supplied via cloud computing, some digital content will always be transmitted to the consumer's device so that they can interact with the digital content product that they have contracted for. This digital content falls within the scope of the definition of digital content as set out in section 2 and, as long as it is provided pursuant to the types of contract set out in section 33 or 46, Chapter 3 applies. The definition of digital content would also cover the digital content supplied to a consumer as the result of a service which produced bespoke digital content, such as a website design service. The Chapter does not apply where a trader supplies a service merely to enable consumers to access digital content, such as Internet or mobile service provision.

167. For contracts involving digital content that has been paid for, Chapter 3 sets out:

- The rights consumers have when they pay a trader to supply digital content to them under contract; these are in effect contractual rights and if they are breached it is a breach of contract;
- when the rights apply;
- what the consumer is entitled to request (and the trader must offer) if these rights are breached: where the trader has no right to supply the digital content the consumer has a right of refund; where other statutory rights about the digital content are breached, the consumer has a right that the trader repairs or replaces the digital content and a subsequent right to a reduction in the price of the digital content; these are the "statutory remedies";
- that the statutory remedies do not prevent the consumer claiming other actions from the trader where they are available according to general contract law (e.g. a claim for damages); and
- that the trader cannot "contract out" of these provisions.

168. For digital content supplied under contract (whether free or paid for), this Chapter sets out:

- that if digital content has damaged the consumer's other digital content, or the consumer's device, and the consumer can prove that the damage was caused because of the trader's lack of reasonable care and skill, then the trader has either to repair the damage or give the consumer some financial compensation for the damage.

169. A legal research paper commissioned by BIS examined core consumer protections relating to digital content and found that it was not clear what, if any, legal rights the consumer has if digital content proves defective or fails to live up to the consumer's expectations. This is because it is not clear whether digital content would be described as goods, services, or something else. The paper concluded that the law in respect of consumer rights in digital content should be clarified[22] and that "in short, digital products should be treated exactly as physical goods, so far as that is possible".

170. The Consumer Contracts (Information, Cancellation and Additional Charges) Regulations 2013 ("the 2013 Regulations"), which implement the CRD, introduce a definition of digital content which is used in this Act. The 2013 Regulations also set out when the consumer has a right to withdraw from digital content contracts that are concluded at a distance (e.g. over the internet), or off premises. They also introduce requirements for digital content traders to provide pre-contractual information on the functionality and interoperability of digital content as well as information on the main characteristics of the digital content (amongst other things). The 2013 Regulations set out the obligation to provide the information but, once it is provided, the Act makes clear that the information will form part of the contract. Where the information is concerned with the digital content itself it will be treated the same as any other description of the digital content.

171. The Government consulted formally on proposals to clarify consumer rights in relation to digital content from July to October 2012 and, since 2010, has also informally consulted a number of consumer and business stakeholders on various aspects of the proposals.

172. The Government published a response to its consultation[23] in June 2013. Most responses to the consultation supported the creation of a new category of digital content in consumer law with a bespoke set of rights and remedies appropriate for the unique nature of digital content.

173. A draft Bill was published in June 2013[24] and scrutinised by the House of Commons Business Innovation and Skills Committee. The Committee published its report in December 2013[25].

What digital content contracts are covered?

*Section 33: **Contracts covered by this chapter***

174. This section sets out which contracts to supply digital content are covered by this Chapter. It clarifies that this Chapter will apply to contracts between a trader and a consumer where a trader agrees to supply digital content that has been:

- Paid for with money,

---

22 Bradgate, R. (2010) 'Consumer rights in digital products: A research report prepared for the UK Department for Business, Innovation and Skills', Institute for Commercial Law Studies, Sheffield and BIS, available here: http://www.bis.gov.uk/assets/biscore/consumer-issues/docs/c/10-1125-consumer-rights-in-digital-products.

23 Consumer Rights Bill Government Response (URN: BIS/13/916)

24 Draft Consumer Rights Bill (URN: BIS/13/925)

25 Draft Consumer Rights Bill; sixth report of session 2013-2014

- Associated with any paid for goods, digital content or services (e.g. free software given away with a paid-for magazine), and not generally available to consumers for free (that is, the consumer must pay something in order to get the digital content), and/or
- Paid for with a facility, such as a token, virtual currency, or gift voucher, that was originally purchased with money (e.g. a magic sword bought within a computer game that was paid for within the game using "jewels" but those jewels were originally purchased with money).

175. Section 46 (Remedy for damage to device or to other digital content) applies to all digital content supplied under contract, including where no money is paid.

176. The Government retains a reserve power to extend the coverage of the digital content provisions to digital content contractually supplied in exchange for something else of value other than money (e.g. in exchange for personal data) in the future, should the Secretary of State be satisfied that there is significant consumer detriment resulting from these sorts of contracts.

What statutory rights are there under a digital content contract?

177. In line with the recommendations of the Bradgate Report, consumers' statutory rights for digital content follow a similar approach to that taken for goods (Chapter 2).

Section 34: Digital content to be of satisfactory quality

178. This section requires that digital content sold to consumers must be of satisfactory quality according to the expectations of a reasonable person. There are several different factors that will affect whether the quality expectations of a reasonable person are met. These are any description of the digital content, the price paid as well as any other relevant circumstances (which includes any public statement about the characteristics of the digital content made by the trader or the manufacturer). This means that, as with goods, this quality standard is flexible to allow for the many different types of digital content. For example, the reasonable expectations of quality for a 69p app would not be as high as for one worth £5.99.

179. The section sets out in *subsection (3)* that the state and condition of the digital content is always an aspect of quality and sets out other matters that can be aspects of quality for the purposes of assessing whether the digital content is satisfactory – fitness for the purposes for which the type of digital content in question is usually supplied; freedom from minor defects, safety and durability (e.g. the lifespan of the digital content). A reasonable person's expectations as to quality are likely to vary according to the nature of the content and some aspects of quality set out in subsection (3) may not be relevant in particular cases. So for example a reasonable person might expect a simple music file to be free from minor defects so that a track which failed to play to the end would not be of satisfactory quality. However, it is the norm to encounter some bugs in a complex game or piece of software on release so a reasonable person might not expect that type of digital content to be free from minor defects. Consequently the application of the quality aspect "freedom from minor defects" to digital content will depend on reasonable expectations as to quality.

180. As with goods, quality does not refer to subjective judgements as to the artistic value of the content itself (e.g. whether or not a book was interesting or well written).

181. Digital content will not be in breach of this section if the consumer was made aware of the aspect of the digital content that makes it unsatisfactory before the contract was concluded – either because it was specifically drawn to their attention or would have been apparent from inspection of the digital content or a trial version. These provisions and those relating to public statements about specific characteristics of the digital content are the same as those for goods (section 9).

Section 35: Digital content to be fit for a particular purpose

182. If the consumer specifies that the digital content will be used for a particular purpose, the digital content must be fit for that particular purpose. This section corresponds to section 10 in relation to goods. For example, if a consumer tells a trader he wants a piece of educational software so that his/her pre-school child can use it then, if it is only suitable for an older child, it would not be fit for that particular purpose (i.e. use by a pre-school child). The section states that the consumer must "make known" to the trader the particular purpose for which it is intended. This implies that the trader must be aware of the consumer's intentions. For example, an email sent to a trader immediately before downloading an app is unlikely to fulfil the "makes known" requirement, whereas an email discussion with a trader would.

183. *Subsection (2)* covers digital content supplied that is sold to a trader by a credit broker but the consumer does all the negotiations with the credit broker. For example, a consumer may talk to a salesperson working for a particular shop about which software would be appropriate to edit a film they are making on their personal computer. The consumer may then buy the digital content on a payment plan (paying in instalments) from a finance company introduced by the shop's salesperson. What may actually happen here is that the store sells the digital content to the finance company who then sells it to the consumer. This section makes sure that the digital content can be held to be fit for the purpose the consumer told the credit broker (i.e. the shop's salesperson), even though the consumer does not contract with the shop directly.

Section 36: Digital content to be as described

184. The right for digital content to be as described is similar to the right for goods (section 11). Section 36 clarifies that the digital content must match any description of it given by the trader to the consumer. This is an important right in the digital content context where people may not be able to view the digital content before buying the full version. Even when the digital content matches a trial version, if it does not meet the description (where they differ), then the digital content will be in breach of this section.

185. The policy intention is that matching the description should mean that the digital content should at least do what it is described as doing. It is not intended that "matches the description" should mean that the digital content must be exactly the same in every aspect. This section would not, for example prevent the digital content going beyond the description, as long as it also continues to match the description. This is particularly relevant for updates that may enhance features or add new features. As clarified in section 40, as long as the digital content continued to match the original product description and conform to the pre-contractual information provided by the trader, improved or additional features would not breach this right.

186. The Consumer Contracts (Information, Cancellation and Additional Charges) Regulations 2013 require traders to provide certain information to consumers before consumers are bound by a contract. The type of information that is required can be split into two categories: information about the digital content (the main characteristics, interoperability and functionality) and other information (e.g. the trader's name and address). In order to implement the obligation to enforce these information requirements the Act makes clear that pre-contractual information will form part of the contract. This section makes clear that the former type of information (about the main characteristics of the digital content or the functionality or interoperability) also forms part of the description.

187. *Subsection (4)* provides that changes to information given pre-contractually about the digital content are only effective when expressly agreed between the consumer and the trader (although it may not be necessary to do so where the pre-contract information itself reflects the fact that the particular potential changes envisaged may be made). That is, if a trader and consumer do not expressly agree the change to the information then if the digital content provided was not in line with this information, this would be

a breach of this section. Conversely, if the trader and consumer do expressly agree a change to the description of the digital content, the consumer would not subsequently be entitled to a remedy if the digital content did not meet the original description but did meet the agreed, changed description.

*Section 37: **Other pre-contract information included in the contract***

188. This section establishes that the other type of information described above (e.g. information on the trader's name and address) provided by the trader pursuant to the obligation in the 2013 Regulations also forms part of the contract between the trader and the consumer. Like the provisions covered in paragraph 71 above, this implements the obligation to enforce relevant parts of the 2013 Regulations.

189. *Subsection (3)* provides that changes to this information are only effective when expressly agreed between the consumer and the trader (although it may not be necessary to do so where the pre-contract information itself reflects the fact that the particular potential changes envisaged may be made).

*Section 38: **No other requirement to treat term about quality or fitness as included***

190. The section makes clear that no other terms about quality or fitness can be implied into the contract. Express terms (that is those that are expressly agreed and set out in the contract) about quality and fitness can be included. Furthermore, if another piece of legislation exists which implies terms into contracts for digital content, these too can be included in the contract (this section does not prevent those being included).

*Section 39: **Supply by transmission and facilities for continued transmission***

191. This section concerns rights that apply when in order to access digital content it is transmitted to the consumer (for example, where digital content is bought or used via the internet or through a satellite transmission) and makes clear that digital content must be of satisfactory quality, fit for a particular purpose and as described at the point when it reaches either the consumer's device or, if earlier, a trader with whom the consumer has contracted, such as an internet service provider or mobile network operator.

192. Digital content can be supplied on a tangible medium (e.g. on a disk or preloaded on a device or embedded within other goods such as a washing machine which relies on software for its programming) or in other ways, such as through streaming or downloading. When it is not supplied on a tangible medium, it will usually travel through one or more intermediaries before it reaches the consumer's device. Some of these intermediaries, for example an Internet Service Provider ("ISP"), have been chosen by and are within the contractual control of the consumer. Other intermediaries, however, will be within the contractual control of the trader, or under arrangements initiated by the trader. For example, a supplier of streamed movies (the trader) may contract with a content delivery network who will deliver the data from the trader's server to the ISPs who will then deliver the content to the consumer.

193. *Subsection (2)* provides that the trader (T) from whom the consumer purchased the digital content supplies the content at the point that it reaches either the consumer's device (for example, directly to a consumer's satellite dish) or an independent trader within the contractual control of the consumer (such as an ISP), whichever is sooner. T is responsible for ensuring that it meets all the relevant quality standards. A trader which is in the contractual control of the consumer and which only provides a service by which the digital content reaches the consumer is not providing digital content for the purposes of Chapter 3 (see section 33(4)) but may be subject to the provision in Chapter 4 (Services)).

194. Where digital content fails to meet the quality standards because of a problem with the consumer's device or with the delivery service supplied by an independent trader with whom the consumer has contracted (e.g. ISP, mobile network provider, cable provider),

T would not be liable for the failure to meet the quality standards as that trader (T) cannot be at fault in any way for the problem and has no way of rectifying it. If the problem is with the consumer's network access provider, then this service provider is liable under the services provision of the Act if, for example, the service is not provided with reasonable care and skill (see Chapter 4). However, where the digital content fails to meet the quality standards because of a problem for which T or an intermediary in the contractual control of T (either directly or indirectly) is responsible, then T will be liable. This is similar to the rules on the passing of risk for goods (section 29) which provide that the trader carries the risk for the goods purchased until they come into the physical possession of the consumer, unless the delivery is arranged by the consumer in which case the consumer takes the risk for the delivery of the goods.

195. *Subsections (3) to (7)* apply to digital content where use of the content in line with the contract requires some digital content to be transferred via the internet between the consumer's device and a server (processing facility) operated by or within the contractual control of T. Examples of this type of digital content would be massively multiplayer online games ("MMOs") and software accessed on the Cloud such as a music streaming facility. *Subsection (5)* provides that for such types of digital content, the consumer should be able to use their digital content in the way described for a reasonable period of time. Where there is an express term in the contract relating to a specific period of time for the use of the digital content in this manner, the express term would apply (e.g. if a consumer expressly pays for 48 hours access to an online journal or for a one month trial period for an MMO game). *Subsection (7)* provides that breach of this provision will give the consumer access to the remedies under section 42. *Subsection (6)* also provides that for these types of contracts for digital content, the quality rights set out in sections 34 to 36 (satisfactory quality, fitness for purpose and meeting the description), should apply to the digital content for that period of time.

*Section 40: **Quality, fitness and description of content supplied subject to modifications***

196. This section reflects a unique issue for digital content in that manufacturers and traders are technically able to change or update digital content after the initial provision of the digital content. This may be set out in the terms and conditions of the licence. In the majority of cases, this is to the benefit of consumers and often includes important updates to the digital content. Requiring consent for every update would create problems for business, both due to the logistics of contacting every consumer and getting their consent and the problems that would arise when some consumers do not accept updates, thus resulting in many different versions of software in circulation and unnecessary disputes with consumers when digital content stops working due to lack of updates.

197. This section therefore does not prevent a trader or a third party (such as the digital content manufacturer) updating digital content, as long as the contract stated that such updates would be supplied. However, such contract terms could be assessable for fairness under Part 2 (Unfair Terms). Furthermore, following any updates, the digital content must still meet the quality rights, (i.e. it must still be of satisfactory quality, be fit for purpose and match the description given). This does not prevent new features from being added or existing features from being enhanced, as long as the digital content continues to match the description and conform to the pre-contractual information provided by the trader. *Subsection (3)* makes clear that the time period for bringing a claim begins when the digital content was first supplied notwithstanding the fact that the modification itself must have occurred some time after the original supply. This means that any claim for breach of this provision must be brought within 6 years of the date the digital content was first supplied.

198. It is for a consumer to prove that the digital content is faulty. Where a consumer has not identified a fault (and therefore not requested a repair or replacement), but a general

update is sent in any case to the consumer, this does not necessarily mean that the quality rights were breached nor that the update constitutes a repair or replacement.

Section 41: Trader's right to supply digital content

199. This section clarifies that a trader must have the right to supply the digital content to the consumer. Often where a consumer buys digital content from a trader there will be other traders who have rights over the digital content, particularly intellectual property rights.

200. This section is slightly different to the equivalent section for goods (section 17) to reflect the fact that (unless the contract states otherwise) the trader does not usually pass on (or sell) all property rights of the digital content (e.g. the ownership of any intellectual property rights to the digital content) to the consumer. More usually, the trader passes on a limited right to use the digital content in certain defined circumstances. The ownership of any rights to the digital content usually stays with the rights holder (usually the originator of the digital content).

201. If the trader does not have the right to supply the digital content at all, the consumer will be entitled to a refund (see section 45).

What remedies are there if statutory rights under a digital content contract are not met?

202. As set out above, Chapter 3 largely only covers those contracts where the consumer has paid some money towards the provision of digital content.

203. This, and following provisions, set out the remedies available to consumers: what consumers are entitled to if the statutory rights are not met.

Section 42: Consumer's rights to enforce terms about digital content

204. If the digital content is not of satisfactory quality, fit for purpose, or does not match the description, the digital content will not conform to the contract. If the digital content does not conform to the contract, the consumer is entitled to require that the trader repairs or replaces the digital content. They can also be entitled to a reduction in price. These two types of remedy are similar to some of those available to consumers of goods, with the notable difference that there is no right to reject digital content as there is when goods do not conform to with the contract (except where the digital content is included in goods – see section 16). The way the remedies fit together is also similar to the goods provisions- if the consumer asks for the digital content to be repaired or replaced, a trader must do so within a reasonable time and without causing significant inconvenience to a consumer. Here, there is a difference compared to the corresponding sections in relation to goods: for goods there are strict limits on the numbers of repairs or replacements a trader can provide (section 24(5)(a) sets out that after one repair or one replacement the trader must offer the consumer some money back). This is because it is the nature of some forms of digital content (such as games) that they may contain a few "bugs" on release. Some consumers will request repairs in relation to the bugs whereas, for the majority of consumers, the same bugs will be fixed by updates which they agreed to in the contract but did not specifically request. Restricting the number of repairs could create an incentive for some consumers to report minor problems with the digital content in order to accumulate a target number of 'repairs' and thus proceed to a price reduction. A strict limit on the number of repairs allowable could therefore have the effect of restricting the availability of this type of product or raising its cost to consumers. However, it is possible that a consumer will be caused "significant inconvenience" after a single repair or replacement.

205. Section 42 does not include a "right to reject" (that is to say, a right to terminate the contract and obtain a refund) substandard digital content. The reason for this contrast with the goods remedies (see section 19) is because digital content cannot be returned in any meaningful sense. However for digital content sold on a tangible medium (e.g.

on a disk or as part of a digital camera), section 16 provides that, where the digital content is substandard (as judged against the digital content quality rights), it will render the goods faulty and so the goods remedies apply. *Subsection (3)* refers back to this section 16 so that consumers who may go directly to the Chapter of the Act that deals with contracts for the supply of digital content will know that they may also have rights under the Chapter that sets out their rights under contracts for the supply of goods. What section 16 makes clear is that consumers do have the right to reject substandard digital content sold on a tangible medium. It also means that there would be strict limits on the number of repairs or replacements that the consumer is required to accept before moving to a price reduction or the final right to reject.

206. Section 42(4) sets out the remedy that applies if the pre-contract information provided pursuant to section 37 is not complied with. This remedy is similar to the remedy of a price reduction (see paragraph 214 below) but as explained below we expect that a price reduction will usually be calculated on the basis of the difference in value between the digital content the consumer receives and what they actually paid. Given that section 37 concerns information that does not describe the digital content (such as the trader's name and address), if it is breached it is unlikely to affect the value of the digital content received and therefore it would not fit with the way it is anticipated a price reduction would be calculated. This subsection therefore provides that a consumer has the right to recover any costs which they incurred as a result of the breach, which could be any amount up to the full price of the digital content (so they could receive a full refund in appropriate cases). This applies equally to a facility for which money has been paid, such as a token, virtual currency, or gift voucher, that was originally purchased with money. Where the consumer has not incurred costs but has suffered other losses as a result of this breach, it may be open to them to claim damages in breach of contract (see below), although it is unlikely that these damages would amount to a significant amount.

207. This section (and sections 43 and 44) does not prevent the consumer seeking other remedies available to them. As set out in paragraph 167 above, the terms that are to be treated as included in the contract in sections 34-37 are contractual terms and if they are not met it means there is a breach of contract. The common law (that is, law that is set out in cases decided by judges) already provides certain remedies for breach of contract. This section serves as a reminder that the consumer may – instead of (or, in some cases, in addition to) pursuing the statutory remedies set out in this section (as explained further in subsequent sections) seek common law (and other) remedies of damages, specific performance or in Scotland specific implement but not so as to recover twice for the same loss.

208. "Damages" refers to the common law remedy of financial compensation paid by one party to the other. For example, where a trader is in breach of a term that this Part requires to be treated as included in a contract, the court may order the trader to pay damages to the consumer. Generally, an award of damages for breach of contract is intended to compensate the injured party for loss suffered. In some, less frequent, cases the court may award damages which go beyond simply compensating the consumer for loss suffered – e.g. a court can sometimes award nominal damages, where there is a breach of contract but no loss, or aggravated damages to compensate for mental distress. For a breach of a term that this Part requires to be treated as included in the contract, the general rule is that damages are intended to put the consumer in the same position as if there had not been a breach. The level of damages awarded will depend on the specific circumstances and the term which the trader has breached. Typically, damages would cover the estimated loss directly resulting from the breach, in the ordinary course of events. This would generally be the difference between the value of the goods, service or digital content received by the consumer and the value had there not been a breach. There are legal tests to be satisfied for a consumer to recover damages: a person can only recover damages for loss which was caused by the breach (of the term required by the Act) and which was sufficiently foreseeable; and the consumer cannot recover for loss which they could reasonably have acted to limit or mitigate.

209. "Specific performance" is a direction a court can make, to compel a party to perform their obligations under a contract. It is an equitable remedy, meaning it is not available to consumers as a right, but at the court's discretion. It will not be ordered if damages (see above) are adequate to compensate the consumer – generally, damages will be adequate unless the subject matter of the contract is unique as the consumer can use damages to buy a replacement. "Specific implement" is similar to "specific performance" for Scotland, and there are likewise specific circumstances where that may be used. In referring to specific performance or specific implement, this section does not seek to codify the law as to when specific performance or specific implement might be available, but the references serve as a reminder that it may be an alternative remedy to the statutory remedies. Section 58 gives more detail on the powers of the court in proceedings where a remedy is sought.

210. As is the normal position, the person who asserts a fault has to prove it. Therefore the burden of proof for proving digital content is faulty, as with goods and services, is on the consumer. However, during the first six months following the purchase if the consumer can prove that the digital content was faulty (it is not of satisfactory quality or does not meet the particular purpose the consumer wanted it for or it does not meet the description) it is assumed that the fault was present on the day the digital content was supplied unless this is inconsistent with the type of alleged fault or can be proven otherwise by the trader.

Section 43: ***Right to repair or replacement***

211. A repair is not necessarily the same as an update to which section 40 applies. A repair means bringing the digital content into conformity with the contract – that is there must first be a breach of contract (the consumer must prove that the digital content does not meet the quality standards set in out in sections 34, 35 or 36 - satisfactory quality, fitness for purpose and meets the description) and then the repair must make the digital content meet those standards. A repair (in response to a request from a consumer) may, in practice, be in the form of an update. Repairing digital content means bringing it back into conformity with the contract. If an update resolves a fault in this way, then it can be a repair (i.e. a repair does not have to be a bespoke solution). A repair or replacement has to be provided within a reasonable time or without significant inconvenience to the consumer.

212. A consumer cannot require the trader to repair or replace the digital content if it is impossible or if repair is disproportionate to replacement or vice versa. If repair or replacement is not provided within a reasonable time or without causing significant inconvenience to the consumer or is impossible, a consumer is entitled to a reduction in price. The reduction will be of an appropriate amount depending on the circumstances of each individual case.

213. For example, a downloaded music file is very low cost to the trader and can be delivered very quickly, and a replacement file would similarly be very quick and easy to provide. In this example, therefore, a reasonable time would be very short and any measure of inconvenience would similarly be very low. However, for an expensive, complicated piece of software which may require a patch to bring it in line with the contract (i.e. it may need to be repaired rather than replaced) the process might be expected to take longer. But, if the digital content was obtained with a specific purpose in mind, for example, when a consumer has paid an extra amount to have early access to an online multi-user game but the server crashed and so the consumer was not able to access the game early, a repair or replacement may not be possible so the consumer would be entitled to a price reduction of an appropriate amount.

Section 44: ***Right to price reduction***

214. Section 44 sets out the circumstances in which the consumer is entitled to a price reduction and establishes that the price reduction could be as much as a full refund or

the full amount they already paid (if they had only paid in part for the digital content). What is an appropriate amount will depend on the circumstances. For example, for digital content such as a film that is fundamentally substandard and fails to play at all, this may be for a 100% refund because the consumer will have obtained no benefit or no substantial or meaningful benefit from the film. In contrast, for a game which the consumer has played for five months and which is exhibiting a minor bug at a later stage in the game play (e.g. a character "floats" instead of "runs"), the consumer has already had some enjoyment from playing the game and the bug does not prevent the game from being played, the appropriate amount might be quite a small proportion of the amount paid. If a single film failed to stream satisfactorily, as part of a monthly subscription, the appropriate amount may reflect the portion of the monthly subscription that could be ascribed to that film. For free digital content given away with, for example, a paid-for magazine, any price reduction would reflect the portion of the price paid that could be ascribed to the digital content instead of the magazine. We expect the reduction in price here to reflect the difference in value between what the consumer paid for the content and what they actually receive.

215. *Subsection (4)* requires a trader to provide any refund due to the consumer without undue delay and at the latest within 14 days from when the trader agrees the consumer is entitled to it. *Subsection (5)* makes clear that the refund must be given using the same means of payment as the consumer used to pay for the digital content, unless the consumer expressly agrees otherwise. If a consumer has paid a trader money to buy in-game currencies (a virtual currency) that can then only be used to buy other digital content from that trader, any digital content bought using the virtual currencies would still be covered by the digital content quality standards in out in sections 34, 35 or 36 (satisfactory quality, fitness for purpose and meets the description) by virtue of section 33(3). However, subsection (5) does not mean that a trader can refund the consumer by giving them back the virtual currency. Rather, to satisfy this requirement a trader must give the consumer back the money originally paid for the in-game currency, using the means of payment that the consumer used to buy that in-game currency (unless the consumer expressly agrees otherwise). However, digital currencies (or cryptocurrencies) that can be used in a variety of transactions with a number of traders, and exchanged for real money, are much more akin to real money (*e.g.* bitcoins). Where the consumer uses these types of digital currency to pay for digital content, the trader can (and must, unless the consumer agrees) repay the consumer in the digital currency. The trader cannot charge the consumer a fee for the payment of the refund.

Section 45: Right to a refund

216. In relation to this section, if the trader's right to supply the digital content (section 41) is breached, the consumer has a right to a full refund. Section 45 does not apply in any other cases (such as a breach of the quality rights). There is no corresponding duty for the consumer to return or delete the digital content for the following reasons. Firstly, the concept of return does not easily sit with digital content (data produced and supplied in digital form) and therefore to provide for a return of the digital content would not be practical; and many consumers would find it difficult to properly delete the digital content[26]. In relation to intellectual property rights, there are other rules that protect these property rights and the Act's provisions in no way undermine those rules. Indeed, if anything, the provisions taken as a whole would support the intellectual property rights of others, since they will act as a disincentive to traders to supply digital content where they do not have the right to do so.

217. *Subsection (2)* of section 45 provides that, where the digital content that the trader did not have the right to supply was only part of the contract (e.g. a single film supplied as part of a subscription package), the refund would not be of the full amount paid, but an appropriate amount paid relating only to the portion of digital content affected.

---

26 Where digital content is provided on a disk or other tangible media, different rules apply

218. Once the trader agrees a refund is due, the payment must be made without undue delay and at the latest within 14 calendar days. The refund must be in the same form as the original payment unless the consumer agrees otherwise. So for example if the consumer paid by credit card the refund should be to their credit card, unless the consumer agrees that a cheque is acceptable (see paragraph 215 for the situations where digital content has been paid for with in-game or digital currency). The trader cannot charge the consumer a fee for the payment of the refund.

Compensation for damage to device or to other digital content

Section 46: Remedy for damage to device or to other digital content

219. Currently, if a consumer downloads some software that contains a virus, he/she could seek to make a negligence claim against the trader if the virus caused loss or damage to the consumer's device or other digital content; claiming that the trader breached a duty of care and skill which caused the consumer loss. This may not be obvious to consumers, however, and this type of negligence claim does not have statutory underpinning. The intention behind this section is therefore to engage the principles behind a negligence claim but limit the type of loss that can be claimed. This section applies to all digital content contractually supplied, whether paid for with money, or free (as long as it is provided pursuant to a contract).

220. If the consumer can demonstrate that the digital content caused damage to the consumer's device or other digital content and the damage was caused because trader failed to use reasonable care and skill to prevent it, then the consumer is entitled to a remedy. The trader can either offer either to repair the damage (as long as that can be done within a reasonable time and without significantly inconveniencing the consumer), or to financially compensate the consumer for the damage. Once the trader agrees the consumer is entitled to compensation, the payment must be made without undue delay and at the latest within 14 calendar days. The trader cannot charge the consumer a fee for the payment of the compensation

221. What constitutes "reasonable care and skill" will be judged against the standards of the profession. For example, it would not generally be reasonable to expect a trader to check every single possible configuration on a consumer's device before providing digital content. However, if the trader has not done something that other traders would do and this has caused damage, it is unlikely to meet the standard of reasonable care and skill. What is reasonable will also depend on the particular circumstances. For example, if an update is an emergency update in response to a security threat, then it may be that the necessary standard of care would be considered lower than the standard that would be reasonable for routine updates designed to fix bugs.

222. A negligence case could still be taken instead of the consumer claiming under this section.

223. In summary, the remedies that apply for breach of the consumer's statutory rights are as follows:

Consumer's statutory rights being breached	***Remedies that may apply***
Digital content to be of satisfactory quality (section 34)	• The right to repair or replacement (section 43) • If repair or replacement are not possible or do not resolve the fault within a reasonable time or without causing significant inconvenience to the consumer the right to a price reduction (section 44)
Digital content to be fit for particular purpose (section 35)	• The right to repair or replacement (section 43)

Consumer's statutory rights being breached	***Remedies that may apply***
	• If repair or replacement are not possible or do not resolve the fault within a reasonable time or without causing significant inconvenience to the consumer, the right to a price reduction (section 44)
Digital content to be as described (section 36)	• The right to repair or replacement (section 43) • If repair or replacement are not possible or do not resolve the fault within a reasonable time or without causing significant inconvenience to the consumer, the right to a price reduction (section 44)
Other pre-contractual information (section 37)	• The right to recover costs incurred as a result of the breach (section 42)
Trader's right to supply digital content (section 41)	• The right to a refund (section 45)
Remedy for damage to device or other digital content (section 46)	The trader must either: • repair the damage; or • compensate the consumer with an appropriate payment (section 46)

Can a trader contract out of statutory rights and remedies under a digital content contract?

Section 47: Liability that cannot be excluded or restricted

224. This section prevents a trader "contracting out" of the provisions in sections 34, 35, 36, 37, and 41. A trader can exclude or restrict their liability arising under section 46 (remedy for damage to device or to other digital content) to the extent that any limitation or exclusion is fair. Any such exclusions would be subject to section 62 (requirement for contract terms and notices to be fair).

225. Many forms of digital content are supplied subject to an End User Licence Agreement ("EULA"). This is because when a consumer contracts for digital content - for example software - it is usually protected by intellectual property law and the consumer needs the intellectual property owner's permission, or licence, to use it. These EULAs may therefore set out the consumer's right to use the digital content. EULAs may also contain terms relating to the quality of the digital content or terms limiting the trader's liability for remedies for faulty digital content. The Law Commissions[27] suggest that some EULAs may have contractual status, for example the research suggests that a court would almost certainly find that those EULAs known as "click-wrap licences", where the consumer has to tick a box to agree terms and conditions before buying a download, were contractual. This may mean that where a consumer has bought digital content from a retailer, as well as having a contract with the retailer, they may have a separate contract with the intellectual property rights holder. As long as the consumer has paid for the digital content (see section 33), the digital content will be subject to the provisions of Chapter 3, and under section 47, the trader from whom the consumer bought the digital content cannot exclude or restrict liability for the rights in Chapter 3 - the consumer would always be able to enforce these rights against the trader from whom they bought the digital content. If there is a contract between the intellectual property rights holder and the consumer, for example the "click wrapped licence" in the example set out above, but the consumer paid no money to the licence holder directly, it is unlikely they could

27 http://lawcommission.justice.gov.uk/docs/unfair_terms_in_consumer_contracts_appendices.pdf

enforce their rights in Chapter 3 against the rights holder since the contracts would not fall within the scope of section 33. However, these contracts would be subject to Part 2 of the Act and any terms in them relating to limiting liability could be held to be unfair. This is also true of other types of EULA such as those known as "shrink-wrap" or "browse-wrap" licences which may not have contractual status but may alternatively be consumer notices. Such consumer notices would be subject to the provisions in Part 2, but the rights set out under Part 1 would not apply since there is no contract.

226. This section also provides that an agreement to submit disputes to arbitration is not covered by this bar on excluding or restricting liability. It should be noted however that paragraph 20 of Schedule 2 makes clear that a term requiring the consumer to take disputes exclusively to arbitration may be regarded as unfair. Furthermore, the Arbitration Act 1996 provides that a term which constitutes an arbitration agreement is automatically unfair under Part 2 of the Act (once in force) if the claim is for less than an amount specified in an Order made under section 91 of the Arbitration Act. This amount is currently set at £5000 in the Unfair Arbitration Agreements (Specified Amount) Order 1999 (SI 1999/2167). It is possible that this amount may change from time to time.

Chapter 4 **Services**

Summary and Background

227. Chapter 4 concerns contracts where a trader supplies a service to a consumer. It sets out:

- the rights a consumer has when a trader provides a service to them under contract; these are, in effect, contractual rights and if they are breached it is therefore a breach of contract;
- what the consumer is entitled to request (and the trader must offer) if these rights are breached: that the trader re-performs the service or where that is not possible or feasible provides a reduction in the price paid for the service (we refer to these as "statutory remedies");
- that the statutory remedies do not prevent the consumer claiming other actions from the trader where they are available according to general contract law (e.g. a claim for damages, termination of the contract); and
- that the trader cannot, in effect, limit its liability for less than the contract price.

228. Chapter 4 applies to all service sectors except where they are expressly excluded from one or all of its provisions. The provisions in this Chapter do not cover contracts of employment or apprenticeships and, where there is legislation that gives more detailed provision about rights or duties of particular services, that legislation will take precedence over the provisions in this Chapter. This Chapter also partially implements Articles 5 and 6 of the CRD; however certain sectors such as financial and gambling services are exempt from those provisions.

229. Currently (that is, until Chapter 4 comes into force) the SGSA provides some protection for recipients of services (whether they are consumers or not) in England, Wales and Northern Ireland (its provisions on services do not extend to Scotland). It sets out that a business supplier of a service must provide that service with 'reasonable care and skill' and, if the time and charge have not been agreed, the service must be provided within a 'reasonable time' and at a 'reasonable charge'. The way it does this is by saying that these matters are "implied terms" of a contract. Implied terms are terms that are not expressly set out in a contract (those expressly set out in a contract are called "express terms"). The effect of this is that, even if these matters are not expressly set out in the contract, these implied terms will still form part of the contract and a business supplier of a service must comply with them, unless they are excluded.

230. At the moment, there are no statutory remedies for breach of the SGSA in respect of its provisions relating solely to services.

231. Section 60 and Schedule 1 make provision for how this new legislation impacts on existing legislation. The SGSA will continue to apply to contracts between businesses.

232. Chapter 4 does not cover all legal rights and obligations surrounding the provision of services, for example there is a large amount of sector specific legislation that will affect contracts between traders and consumers.

233. In addition, the 2013 Regulations provide that, for all types of consumer contracts within scope, including most service contracts, a trader must provide certain information to the consumer before the contract is entered into.

234. In 2010, BIS commissioned a report, entitled 'Consolidation and Simplification of UK Consumer Law[28]' to examine how existing consumer law might be consolidated and simplified to make it more accessible to consumers, business and their advisers. That report recommended that consumer contract law would be improved if many of the provisions could be brought together into a single consumer contract law that, so far as appropriate, subjected all consumer supply contracts to the same rights and remedies. The report recommended that this be done using simpler language, such as avoiding specialist legal language including references to 'implied terms'. The report suggested that remedies for services should be made clearer and more accessible by incorporating them into the legislation.

235. Following the 2010 report, BIS carried out a consultation, from 13 July to 5 October 2012, into proposals for reform of the law regarding contractual supplies to consumers of services, as well as of goods and digital content. This consultation covered most of the recommendations of the 2010 Report, including how to present 'implied terms' in easier and more accessible language, whether to introduce statutory remedies and whether to introduce a new 'satisfactory quality' standard for all or certain types of services.

236. Following the consultation, BIS published a government response. Most responses to the consultation supported simplification and removal of difficult to understand phrases, and the introduction of statutory remedies for when things go wrong in the provision of services. A draft Bill was published in June 2013[29] and scrutinised by the House of Commons Business Innovation and Skills Committee. The Committee published its report in December 2013[30].

What services contracts are covered?

Section 48: Contracts covered by this Chapter

237. This section sets out which contracts are covered by Chapter 4. It follows the structure of the corresponding provision of the SGSA but makes clear that Chapter 4 is only concerned with contracts where a trader provides a service to a consumer (and not where a trader provides a service to another trader or where a consumer provides a service to a consumer or a trader). It also sets out that contracts of employment are not covered by this Chapter.

238. In contrast to the relevant Part of the SGSA, Chapter 4, like the rest of the Act, applies to the whole of the UK, including Scotland.

239. In keeping with the SGSA, Chapter 4 also covers contracts in which the trader does not undertake to provide the service personally, but rather uses a subcontractor (or agent)

---

28 The report was authored by Professor Geraint Howells and Professor Christian Twigg-Flesner available at: https://www.gov.uk/government/uploads/system/uploads/attachment_data/file/31838/10-1255-consolidation-simplification-uk-consumer-law.pdf

29 Draft Consumer Rights Bill (URN: BIS/13/925)

30 Draft Consumer Rights Bill; sixth report of session 2013-2014

to perform the service. For example, a house-building firm may engage a specialist glazing firm to perform part of the work that they have contracted with the consumer to perform, and the house-builder would still be bound by the provisions in this Chapter for the performance of the service by the glazing firm.

240. This section includes a power exercisable by statutory instrument to dis-apply the provisions to a particular service or particular services. There is a similar power in the SGSA, which has been used to dis-apply section 13 (implied term to take reasonable care and skill) of SGSA to the services provided by an advocate in a court or tribunal, by a company director, by a director of a building society and the management of a provident society to that building or provident society and finally to services rendered by an arbitrator in their capacity as such. Contracts of employment are also excluded from the scope of SGSA. Employees are protected by employment specific legislation, such as the Employment Rights Act 1996.

241. This Chapter applies whether the service is supplied immediately or the parties agree that the trader will supply it at a future time.

What statutory rights are there under a services contract?

Section 49: Service to be performed with reasonable care and skill

242. This Section corresponds to section 13 of the SGSA but, as with all the provisions in Part 1 of the Act, it only relates to contracts between traders and consumers, specifically here, where a trader supplies a service to a consumer. It removes the legalistic reference to an 'implied term' that is in the SGSA and simply says that every contract where a trader supplies a service to a consumer includes a term that the service must be performed with reasonable care and skill. The standard that the trader must meet in section 49 and in section 13 of the SGSA however is the same and if the trader does not meet the test of "reasonable care and skill", the trader will be in breach of contract.

243. "Reasonable care and skill" focuses on the way a service has been carried out, rather than the end result of the service. This means that, if a trader has not provided a service with reasonable care and skill, they will be in breach of this right, whatever the end result.

244. This provision does not include a definition of "reasonable care and skill". This is to allow the standard to be flexible between sectors and industries. It is also to reflect that current case law provides guidance on this meaning and, further, that future case law might elaborate on that guidance. It is generally accepted that relevant to whether a person has met the standard of reasonable care and skill are industry standards or codes of practice. The price paid for the service can also be a factor in determining the level of care and skill that needs to be exercised in order to be reasonable. For example, a consumer might expect a lower standard of care and skill from a quick and cheap repair service than from a more expensive and thorough one.

245. For example, if an individual engages a high-cost, specialized gardener to landscape his/her garden, that gardening service must be provided with reasonable care and skill. If the gardener does not cut and treat the grass to the industry standard, it is likely that a court would find that the gardener did not exercise reasonable care and skill and the consumer would have the right to remedies (explained below).

Section 50: Information about the trader or service to be binding

246. This is a new provision in that there is no corresponding provision in the SGSA. It is incorporated here for two reasons:

- Firstly, there may be consumer detriment where a trader may say something to a consumer, which the consumer then relies on, but which the trader later does not comply with. Whilst it may be the case that the proper legal construction is that these statements are validly incorporated into the contract as express terms, a trader may try to argue that they are not contractually bound by the statement; and

- Secondly, for certain contracts, the 2013 Regulations mandate that certain information must be made available by a trader to a consumer before the consumer is bound by a contract. To enable enforcement of those Regulations, the Act makes clear that these pieces of information will form part of the contract – so that the service must be provided as stated in the information - which cannot be altered unless the parties expressly agree otherwise (although it may not be necessary to do so where the pre-contract information itself reflects the fact that the particular potential changes envisaged may be made). This part of the 2013 Regulations aims to ensure that consumers are properly informed of key information before they are bound by a contract. Certain services are excluded from the scope of the 2013 Regulations and therefore from this provision, such as financial and gambling services.

247. Section 50 may be considered in two parts to deal with these two objectives above.

248. Firstly, the section requires that that the trader providing the service must comply with information it has provided, orally or in writing (e.g. a description it has given of the service to be provided), where the consumer has taken this information into account when making any decision about the service (including whether to enter into the contract). This information must be read in the context of everything else in the contract and other information given. This is to prevent the consumer being able to rely on some information, where the trader clearly qualified that information when giving it to the consumer. *Subsection* (2) makes this clear.

249. The information given covers both information about the service and other information the trader gives about the trader itself (e.g. information about its trading practices, such as a commitment to paying its workers the minimum wage). Different remedies apply depending on whether the information is about the service or is other information that the trader gives (see below).

250. Secondly, the section explains that information provided which was required under the 2013 Regulations is also to be treated as included in the contract. Therefore, the trader must comply with the information it has provided or be in breach of contract.

251. For both types of information (that required under 2013 Regulations and information provided by the trader voluntarily) this section also makes clear that the trader and consumer can later agree a change to the contract if, for example, circumstances change. A trader will not however be able to change the effect of this information without the agreement of the consumer, unless the information itself reflects the fact that the particular potential changes envisaged may be made (or, in the case of information provided voluntarily by the trader, the trader otherwise qualified the information on the same occasion as providing it). Variation provisions in a contract between a trader and a consumer must also comply with Part 2 of the Act on unfair terms. For neither type of information can the parties agree a change which would deprive the consumer of his or her rights under this Chapter (see section 57).

252. For example, a consumer invites a trader to their home where they agree a contract for the fitting of windows. The consumer chooses that trader to fit wooden windows on the basis that the trader said that it would install and fully finish the frames. If, after fitting the windows, the fitter would only prime the frame and told the consumer to paint them him/herself, the trader would not have complied with the information it gave the consumer, and which the consumer had taken into account. Under the 2013 Regulations, for services within scope, the trader must give the consumer the "main characteristics" of the service and the service must comply with those characteristics. This is in addition to the right that the service must generally comply with any information given to the consumer by the trader which the consumer takes into account when deciding to enter into the contract

Section 51: Reasonable price to be paid for a service

253. In most cases, a contract will set out the price for the service, and indeed following the 2013 Regulations, traders who are not excluded will be under an obligation to provide information about the price before the consumer is bound by the contract. In addition, the price could be paid up-front when the contract is agreed, in which case the consumer will know the price. If for any reason the price is not known from the outset, this provision sets out that the consumer must pay a reasonable price. What is 'reasonable' is a question of fact. This means that if the question of what is a reasonable price comes before a court and the court makes a decision, the ability of the parties to appeal that decision will be limited once it has been made.

254. This section corresponds to section 15 of the SGSA but updates the language in line with the rest of Part 1.

255. For example, if a home owner engages a plumber to fix an urgent leak, he/she may not take the time to discuss the price before fixing the problem. The price might not be in the contract if the plumber did not know the problem before he/she arrived to fix it. If the leak was fixed in ten minutes and with only a £50 replacement part, £1000 is unlikely to be a reasonable price to pay.

Section 52: Service to be performed within a reasonable time

256. Like the price of the service (discussed above), the time for performance of the service is not always agreed in advance. For situations where a time for performance of the service has not been agreed, this section gives the consumer the right to have the service provided within a reasonable time after the contract is agreed.

257. For example, an individual engages a builder to rebuild a 1 metre high, 25 metre long garden wall. At the outset, the individual agrees the price with the builder, but not a deadline for completion of the work. If, six months later, the work had not been completed, the builder would most likely not have carried out the work within a reasonable time.

258. There is a similar provision in section 14 of the SGSA.

Section 53: Relation to other law on contract terms

259. The provision in this section corresponds to section 16 of the SGSA. It recognises that certain types of contract to provide services are regulated by sector specific legislation (e.g. financial services). In most of those cases, this provision means that the sector specific legislation applies alongside or instead of this Chapter.

260. *Subsection* (1) preserves any enactments or rules of law which impose stricter duties than those imposed by sections 49-52. "Rules of law" means a rule of the common law.

261. *Subsection* (2) means that where Parliament has turned its mind to a particular type of service, and has decided that that service should be subject to particular rules, those rules take precedence over those in the Act. "Enactment" is defined in section 59 to cover primary legislation and also "subordinate legislation", which is defined in the Interpretation Act 1978 as "Orders in Council, orders, rules, regulations, schemes, warrants, byelaws and other instruments made or to be made under any Act".

What remedies are there if statutory rights under a services contract are not met?

Section 54: Consumer's rights to enforce terms about services; section 55: Right to repeat performance; and section 56: Right to price reduction

262. The provisions in these sections set out the remedies available to consumers if the statutory rights set out in Chapter 4 are not met. Section 54 also clarifies that there might

be other remedies available, for example, seeking of damages (which may be available under common law).

263. If the service is not provided with reasonable care and skill (and so breaches the provision in section 49) or where the service is not performed in line with information given about the service (and so in breach of section 50), the service will not conform to the contract. If the service does not conform to the contract, the consumer is entitled to require that the service is properly performed, through it (or part of it) being done again. The consumer can also be entitled to request a reduction in price in certain circumstances. These two statutory remedies are available as alternatives (or, in some cases in addition) to remedies available under common law or equity, for example damages and specific performance (see paragraphs 271-273 below). So a consumer does not have to ask for a statutory remedy of re-performance if they would prefer to seek damages, for example. The two statutory remedies are similar to those available to consumers of goods (in section 19 onwards). The way the remedies fit together is also similar to the regime for goods as set out in Chapter 2 – if the consumer asks for the service to be re-performed, a trader must do so within a reasonable time and without causing significant inconvenience to the consumer. A consumer cannot require re-performance if it is impossible, for example this might apply if the service was time specific. If re-performance is not provided within a reasonable time or without causing significant inconvenience to the consumer or is impossible, the consumer is entitled to a reduction in price. The reduction will be of an appropriate amount depending on the circumstances of each individual case.

264. If the information provided about the trader is not complied with (and there is a breach of section 50), the consumer has the right to a reduction in price of an appropriate amount. This is in addition to potentially having access to remedies at common law and equity (see paragraphs 271-273 below).

265. If the service is not provided within a reasonable time (and so breaches the provision in section 52), the consumer has the right to a reduction in price of an appropriate amount. This is in addition to potentially having access to remedies at common law and equity (see paragraphs 271-273 below).

266. A "reduction in price of an appropriate amount" will normally mean that the price is reduced by the difference in value between the service the consumer paid for and the value of the service as provided. In practice, this will mean that the reduction in price from the full amount takes into account the benefit which the consumer has derived from the service. Depending on the circumstances, the reduction in price could mean a full refund. This could be, for example, where the consumer has derived no benefit from the service and the consumer would have to employ another trader to repeat the service "from scratch" to complete the work.

267. In relation to services, however, there may be some cases consumer is able to ask for a reduction in price even where it may be argued that the value of the service as provided has not been reduced by the breach of the consumer's rights. This could occur, for example, where the trader has not complied with information they gave about themselves. For example, if the trader tells the consumer that they will pay their workers the living wage and this is important to the consumer and a reason why they decided to go with this particular trader, arguably this does not affect the value of the service but the consumer would still have the right to request a reduction of an "appropriate amount" to account for the breach.

268. Where a consumer has the right to ask the trader to re-perform the service the trader must re-perform all or part of the service as needed to bring it into conformity with the contract.

269. Where the consumer has the right to a reduction in price, once the trader and consumer have agreed the consumer is entitled to a reduction in price, any refund for anything paid above the reduced amount must be made without undue delay. In many cases, a trader

will be able to give money back at the time of agreeing that the consumer is entitled to a reduction in price. For example, in a hairdressers, if a consumer had already paid in cash, the owner would be able quickly to provide money back from the till. However, where a refund cannot be given at the time of agreeing that the consumer is entitled to that reduction, the refund must be given without undue delay and within 14 days of that agreement at the latest. For example, for a design service provided online, it may take 3-4 days to process the payment to the consumer. To be without "undue delay" the refund should be given as soon as the trader is able to give it. A factor out of the trader's control, such as a bank processing time, would be unlikely to be considered an "undue delay".

270. The refund must be in the same form as the original payment unless the consumer agrees otherwise. So for example if the consumer paid for the service by credit card the refund should be to their credit card, unless the consumer agrees that a cheque is acceptable. The trader cannot charge the consumer a fee for the payment of the refund.

271. As set out in paragraph 227 above, the terms that are to be treated as included in the contract in sections 49-52 are contractual terms and if they are not met it means there is a breach of contract. The common law (that is, law that is set out in cases decided by judges) already provides certain remedies for breach of contract. Section 54 provides a reminder that the consumer may, instead of (or, in some cases, in addition to) pursuing the statutory remedies set out in this section and subsequent sections, seek common law remedies of damages or treating the contract as at an end where for example the breach is very serious, or the equitable remedy of specific performance or (in Scotland) specific implement.

272. "Damages" refers to the common law remedy of financial compensation paid by one party to the other. For example, where a trader is in breach of a term that this Part requires to be treated as included in a contract, the court may order the trader to pay damages to the consumer. Generally, an award of damages for breach of contract is intended to compensate the injured party for loss suffered. In some, less frequent, cases the court may award damages which go beyond simply compensating the consumer for loss suffered – e.g. a court can sometimes award nominal damages, where there is a breach of contract but no loss, or aggravated damages to compensate for mental distress. For a breach of a term that this Part requires to be treated as included in the contract, the general rule is that damages are intended to put the consumer in the same position as if there had not been a breach. The level of damages awarded will depend on the specific circumstances and the term which the trader has breached. Typically, damages would cover the estimated loss directly resulting from the breach, in the ordinary course of events. This would generally be the difference between the value of the goods, service or digital content received by the consumer and the value had there not been a breach. There are legal tests to be satisfied for a consumer to recover damages: a person can only recover damages for loss which was caused by the breach (of the term required by the Act) and which was sufficiently foreseeable; and the consumer cannot recover for loss which they could reasonably have acted to limit or mitigate.

273. "Specific performance" is a direction a court can make, to compel a party to perform their obligations under a contract. It is an equitable remedy, meaning it is not available to consumers as a right, but at the court's discretion. It will not be ordered if damages (see above) are adequate to compensate the consumer – generally, damages will be adequate unless the subject matter of the contract is unique as the consumer can use damages to buy a replacement. "Specific implement" is similar to "specific performance" for Scotland, and there are likewise specific circumstances where that may be used. In referring to specific performance or specific implement, this section does not seek to codify the law as to when specific performance or specific implement might be available, but the references serve as a reminder that it may be an alternative remedy to the statutory remedies. Section 58 gives more detail on the powers of the court in proceedings where a remedy is sought.

274. In summary (see above and the sections themselves for more detail), the remedies that apply for breach of the consumer's statutory rights are as follows:

Consumers' statutory right being breached	***Remedies that apply***
Service not performed with reasonable care and skill (section 49)	• The right to ask for a repeat performance (sections 54 and 55) • And, if that is impossible, or not done in a reasonable time or without significant inconvenience: • The right to a reduction in price (sections 54 and 56)
Service not performed within a reasonable time (section 52)	• The right to a reduction in price (sections 54 and 56)
Service not performed in-line with information provided concerning the service (section 50)	• The right to ask for a repeat performance (sections 54 and 55) • And, if that is impossible, or not done in a reasonable time without inconvenience: • The right to a reduction in price (sections 54 and 56)
Service not performed in-line with information provided concerning the trader (section 50)	• The right to a reduction in price (sections 54 and 56)

275. For example, a consumer has his/her house treated for subsidence, with a new kitchen floor laid and bedrooms redecorated. But, whilst the bedrooms are fine, in the kitchen the builder has just papered over cracks, and the kitchen floor is uneven. The builder accepts that the job in the kitchen was not done with reasonable care and skill. In this case, the consumer can insist that the builder re-does the relevant work without any extra cost to the consumer. If the builder does not do that within a reasonable time, the consumer would be entitled to a price reduction of an appropriate amount. The amount would reflect that only some of the work was not done with reasonable care and skill.

276. For example, if a decorator is engaged to paint a room in a certain high quality paint, stating in advance that he/she will do so, and the consumer took this into account when deciding whether to enter into the contract with this decorator, and the decorator uses lower quality paint, the consumer would be entitled to have the room repainted in the agreed paint and, if that was impossible or couldn't be done for another (say) ten weeks, the consumer would be entitled to a reduction in price. If the decorator claimed to have a certain qualification and the consumer only wanted to contract with someone with this qualification, which the decorator did not in fact have, the consumer would be entitled to a price reduction. If the decorator were to arrive to paint the room one year after being engaged to do so, that delay would entitle the consumer to a reduction in price. A reduction in price could be of the full amount.

Can a trader contract out of statutory rights and remedies under a services contract?

Section 57: Liability that cannot be excluded or restricted

277. This section addresses "contracting out" of the consumer's statutory rights as established under sections 49, 50, 51 and 52. It also makes clear that a trader cannot limit its liability for breach of these sections to less than the contract price.

278. As regards the consumer's statutory rights as established under section 49 (service to be performed with reasonable care and skill) and section 50 (information about the trader or service to be binding) the trader cannot "contract out" of complying with those rights. That is, the parties cannot agree in their contract that the trader has no responsibility in relation to those rights. They also cannot limit their liability for breach of those sections to less than the contract price.

279. As regards the consumer's statutory rights as established under section 51 (reasonable price to be paid for a service) and section 52 (service to be provided within a reasonable time) the trader can dis-apply these sections by specifying the price (so that section 51 and the default rule which it imposes does not apply) or time (so that section 52 and the default rule which it imposes does not apply) for providing the service. Where these sections do apply, the trader cannot limit their liability for breach of those sections to less than the contract price.

280. Even if a term does not contravene this section (i.e. does not limit its liability to less than the contract price) it is still subject to Part 2 (Unfair Terms).

281. For example, a decorator cannot get around complying with the statutory rights by asking a consumer to sign a contract to paint a room where the contract includes a term such as 'the decorator accepts no responsibility if the paint work is not completed with reasonable care and skill'. If this is in the contract, that term will be invalid.

282. This section also provides that an agreement to submit disputes to arbitration is not covered by the bars on excluding or restricting liability. It should be noted however that paragraph 20 of Schedule 2 makes clear that a term requiring the consumer to take disputes exclusively to arbitration may be regarded as unfair. Furthermore, the Arbitration Act 1996 provides that a term which constitutes an arbitration agreement is automatically unfair (under Part 2 of the Act) if the claim is for less than an amount specified in an Order made under section 91 of the Arbitration Act. This amount is currently set at £5000 in the Unfair Arbitration Agreements (Specified Amount) Order 1999 (SI 1999/2167). It is possible that this amount may change from time to time.

Chapter 5 General and Supplementary Provisions

283. Section 58 sets out powers that a court may use to enforce the remedies of repair, replacement or repeat performance and final right to reject or price reduction (as applicable). *Subsection* (1) sets out the types of dispute between a consumer and trader in which the powers can be used. For goods, the section is similar in effect to section 48E of the SGA and section 11R of the SGSA for contracts between a trader and consumer, but reflects the limits on deduction for use under section 24(9)-(10). This section makes similar provision for services and digital content to that for goods.

284. Paragraphs 104, 209 and 273 above provide explanation of specific performance and specific implement.

285. Under *subsections* (3) and (4), a court may substitute a remedy under the provisions specified in *subsection* (8), in accordance with the hierarchy and conditions to exercising the remedies within the Act. So, for example, in relation to a contract to supply goods, a court could only order price reduction when the consumer had requested repair, if repair and replacement were impossible (as required by section 23(3)).

286. Section 59 provides definitions of terms used in the Act other than the key definitions set out in section 2 and section 60 gives effect to Schedule 1 which details consequential amendments to existing legislation resulting from the implementation of Part 1.

Part 2: Unfair Terms

Background and overview

287. Part 2 of the Act clarifies and consolidates existing consumer legislation on unfair terms.

288. In 2005, the Law Commissions concluded, following an earlier consultation, that the law on unfair contract terms is particularly complex[31]. It is contained in two separate pieces of legislation– the UCTA and the UTCCRs – that have inconsistent and overlapping provisions.

289. The UCTA applies to a broad range of contracts, including those between two businesses, contracts between businesses and consumers and even, to a limited extent, to contracts between two consumers. It applies to individually negotiated as well as non-negotiated terms. It focuses on exclusions, that is to say terms or notices which aim to exclude or restrict liability for: negligence causing death or personal injury; negligence causing other loss; and breach of contract. As a result, for example, traders are not permitted to exclude their liability for negligence causing death or personal injury. Other exclusions are only binding if they meet the 'reasonableness requirement'. Some types of contracts are exempted, for example those relating to insurance contracts, interests in land or, other than in Scotland, intellectual property rights.

290. The UTCCRs implement the Unfair Terms in Consumer Contracts Directive (Council Directive 93/13/EEC) ("UTCCD"), and only apply to non-negotiated (standard term) contract terms between a trader and a consumer. They provide that contract terms must be "fair" and written in "plain, intelligible language". The definition of fairness differs from the reasonableness test in the UCTA, and while overall both pieces of legislation may in some cases achieve a similar effect, they do so in different ways. In their 2005 report, the Law Commissions concluded that the two overlapping and inconsistent pieces of unfair terms legislation have led to complexity and confusion about how the law should be applied.

291. A transposition note setting out how the main elements of this Directive are transposed in the Act is annexed to these explanatory notes – please see Annex B.

292. In 2012, BIS asked the Law Commissions to look again at how the legislation could be clarified in the light of some high profile legal cases. They therefore undertook a consultation in 2012[32], to obtain up-to-date evidence and views on their proposals for reform.

293. The focus of the consultation was on two particular areas:

- contract terms that are exempted from an assessment of fairness by the courts because they concern the essential bargain of the contract – the subject matter and the adequacy of the price (this is commonly referred to as "the exemption"); and
- an indicative and non-exhaustive schedule of types of terms that may be considered unfair (this is commonly referred to as "the grey list").

294. Part 2 consolidates the UCTA and the UTCCRs, to remove conflicting overlapping provisions and, in particular, to clarify and amend the law on the above-mentioned exemption and the "grey list".

What contracts and notices are covered by this Part?

Section 61: Contracts and notices covered by this Part

295. This section sets out the scope of Part 2 of the Act:

- It covers contracts between a trader and a consumer. For ease of reference, trader to consumer contracts are called 'consumer contracts' in this Part.
- Whilst Part 2 concerns contracts, it also includes consumer notices – both contractual and non-contractual consumer notices. A consumer notice includes an announcement or other communication which it is reasonable to assume is intended

31 Their documents can be found at http://lawcommission.justice.gov.uk/areas/unfair-terms-in-contracts.htm
32 ibid

to be read by a consumer. Non-contractual consumer notices (e.g. a sign in a car park) do not include an exchange of something in return for something else of value (known as "consideration") as a contract does.

- This Part does not cover employment contacts, as they are regulated by specific employment legislation.

296. This Part covers terms in End User Licence Agreements to the extent that they are either consumer contracts or consumer notices. Research[33] suggests that some End User Licence Agreements, for example those known as "click-wrap licences", which the consumer must explicitly agree to before they are able to download digital content, may have contractual status. Consumer contracts are subject to the provisions of Part 2 and if they contain terms listed in Schedule 2, those terms are assessable for fairness. Other types of End User Licence Agreements, such as those known as "shrink-wrap" or "browse-wrap" licences, may not have contractual status but may alternatively be consumer notices, and therefore also be subject to the provisions in Part 2. End User Licence Agreements may also set out for the consumer legal provisions in other pieces of legislation, such as those in relation to intellectual property. Section 73 makes clear that the Act's unfair terms provisions do not override legal requirements in other legislation, therefore if a term reflects other law, then it will be exempt from the provisions in Part 2.

What are the general rules about fairness of contract terms and notices?

*Section 62: **Requirement for contract terms and notices to be fair***

297. The effect of this section is that terms used in contracts and notices will only be binding upon the consumer if they are fair. It defines 'unfair' terms as those which put the consumer at a disadvantage, by limiting the consumer's rights or disproportionately increasing their obligations as compared to the trader's rights and obligations.

298. This section also sets out factors that a court should take into account when determining whether a term is fair, notably that it should consider the specific circumstances existing when the term was agreed, other terms in the contract and the nature of the subject matter of the contract. This assessment is known as the 'fairness test' (see also section 63 as regards the list of terms that may be used to assist a court when considering the application of the fairness test).

299. For example, a contract to subscribe to a magazine could contain a term allowing the publisher to cancel the subscription at short notice. In deciding whether this is fair or not, the court could consider issues such as whether the subscriber can also cancel at short notice or obtain a refund if the publisher cancels the contract.

300. *Subsection* (8) explains that terms which are void will still be void regardless of the fairness test explained in this section. Terms which are void may still be subject to the fairness test and found to be unfair, however if they are found to be fair that does not prevent them from being void.

301. This section brings together sections 4 and 11 of the UCTA (for England, Wales and Northern Ireland), sections 17 and 18 of the UCTA (for Scotland), and regulations 5 and 6 of the UTCCRs. This section also implements Articles 3, 4 and 6 of the UTCCD.

*Section 63: **Contract terms which may or must be regarded as unfair***

302. This section introduces Schedule 2, which lists examples of terms which may be regarded as unfair (this list is known as the "grey list"). Schedule 2 is an indicative and non-exhaustive list. The terms on the list are not automatically unfair, but may be used to assist a court when considering the application of the fairness test in section 62 to a

33 http://lawcommission.justice.gov.uk/docs/unfair_terms_in_consumer_contracts_appendices.pdf

particular case. Equally, terms not found on the list in the Schedule may be found by a court to be unfair by application of the fairness test. This section and the Schedule are based on a copy-out of Article 3(3) of, and the Annex to, the UTCCD. Part 2 of the Schedule explains the scope of the list such that terms in Part 2 are not considered as part of the Schedule but are still assessable for fairness unless section 64 or section 73 applies. Part 2 of the "grey list" accounts, for example, for the specific nature of financial services contracts where fluctuations in the market may influence the price.

303. Terms on the "grey list" are assessable for fairness even if they would otherwise qualify for an exemption under section 64. Terms on the "grey list" are assessable even if they are "transparent" and "prominent" as defined in section 64.

304. For example, if a contract to subscribe to a magazine included a term which provided that the publisher, but not the subscriber, could cancel the delivery at short notice, that term may be regarded as unfair, as it is covered by paragraph 7 of the Schedule (which gives a term which authorises "the trader to dissolve the contact on a discretionary basis where the same facility is not granted to the consumer" as an example of a term which may be unfair). This does not mean that the term is automatically unfair, but the court must take this into account when assessing the term under the fairness test in section 62.

305. This reflects the case law of the EU Court of Justice on the effect of the list of terms in the Annex to the UTCCD. In Case C-478/99 *Commission v Sweden* (2002) ECR I-4147, the Court stated:

> "It is not disputed that a term appearing in the list need not necessarily be considered unfair and, conversely, a term that does not appear in the list may none the less be regarded as unfair... In so far as it does not limit the discretion of the national authorities to determine the unfairness of a term, the list contained in the annex to the Directive does not seek to give consumers rights going beyond those that result from Articles 3 to 7 of the Directive... Inasmuch as the list contained in the annex to the Directive is of indicative and illustrative value, it constitutes a source of information both for the national authorities responsible for applying the implementing measures and for individuals affected by those measures.
>
> (paras.20-22)

306. In Case C-472/10 *Nemzeti* (judgment of 26 April 2012) the Court emphasised the importance of the list:

> "If the content of the annex does not suffice in itself to establish automatically the unfair nature of a contested term, it is nevertheless an essential element on which the competent court may base its assessment as to the unfair nature of that term.
>
> (para.26)

307. Part 1 of Schedule 2 is as included in the UTCCRs and in the UTCCD, however the terminology has been brought in-line with the Act as a whole. In addition, three additional items have been added to the list (paragraphs 5, 12 and 14) as recommended by the Law Commissions in their report of March 2013[34].

308. Paragraph 5 adds to the grey list terms of a contract which have the object or effect of requiring that a consumer pay a disproportionate amount if they decide not to continue the contract. In this paragraph the phrase "decides not to conclude or perform" includes where a consumer cancels a contract (and is charged a so-called "termination fee").

309. Paragraph 12 adds to the grey list terms which have the object or effect of allowing the trader to determine the subject matter of the contract after the contract has been agreed with the consumer. In certain circumstances, defined in paragraph 23, this does not apply to contracts which last indefinitely.

---

34 http://lawcommission.justice.gov.uk/docs/unfair_terms_in_consumer_contracts_advice.pdf

310. Paragraph 14 adds to the grey list terms which have the object or effect of allowing the trader to set (for the first time) the price under a contract (or the method for calculating the price), after that contract has been agreed with the consumer. The paragraph expressly provides that, in certain circumstances, defined in paragraphs 23, 24, and 25, it does not apply to contracts which last indefinitely, contracts for the sale of securities and foreign currency (etc), and price index clauses. This is only for the avoidance of doubt, because in most of these situations the price of the contract, or the method for calculating it, will be determined before the contract is agreed, so paragraph 14 would not be relevant.

311. This section also implements Article 15 of the Distance Marketing Directive (Directive 2002/65/EC concerning the distance marketing of consumer financial services, implemented in the UK in the Financial Services (Distance Marketing) Regulations 2004 (SI 2004/2095)). That Directive sets common minimum standards for the information that must be given to a consumer prior to a distance contract for financial services being concluded. There are also provisions for rights of withdrawal ('cancellation rights') in many circumstances, and provisions to protect consumers in relation to misuse of payment cards in connection with distance contracts for financial services, unsolicited supplies of financial services and unsolicited communications about such services. Article 15 provides that any contractual term or condition that puts the burden of proof on the consumer (rather than the trader) to show non-compliance with the Directive is an unfair term.

*Section 64: **Exclusion from assessment of fairness***

312. This section describes how the assessment of fairness of price and subject matter terms in consumer contracts is limited.

313. If a term is of the type listed in Part 1 of Schedule 2, it can be assessed for fairness. Other terms in a consumer contract can be assessed for fairness except to the extent that:

a) they specify the main subject matter of the contract (usually the goods, services or digital content being purchased); or

b) the assessment is of the appropriateness (usually the level) of the price payable under the contract compared with what is supplied under it.

However, if such price or subject matter terms are not transparent and prominent (*e.g.* if they are in the small print) they are assessable for fairness.

314. Then, in order to determine whether it is assessable for fairness, the court will first consider whether a price or subject matter term is transparent and prominent. If such a term is not transparent and prominent (e.g. if it is in the 'small print'), it is assessable for fairness. If the term is transparent and prominent, it is exempt from assessment for fairness.

315. This provision replaces regulation 6(2) of the UTCCRs, and implements the exemption in Article 4(2) of the UTCCD. Regulation 6(2) was considered in *Office of Fair Trading v Abbey National plc* [2009] UKSC 6. The Supreme Court concluded that the concepts of main subject matter and price are to be narrowly construed as "*the two sides of the* quid pro quo *inherent in any consumer contract*", that is, the goods or service that the trader agrees to provide, and the price that the consumer agrees to pay (Lord Walker at para.39). Lord Walker explained that the fact that other types of price terms appeared on the grey list reinforced this narrow construction of the exemption:

"This House's decision in First National Bank shows that not every term that is in some way linked to monetary consideration falls within Regulation 6(2)(b). Paras (d), (e), (f) and (l) of the "grey list" in Schedule 2 to the 1999 Regulations are an illustration of that. (Lord Walker, para.43)

316. Reflecting this case law, the effect of this section is that, if a term concerns other aspects of the price other than the amount, for example the timing of payment, the term may be assessed for fairness, but the amount of the price cannot be assessed (if it is transparent and prominent as defined here).

317. For example, if an individual contracts with a catering company to provide a buffet lunch, and the contract includes a term that the individual will pay £100 for a 3 course meal, the court cannot look at whether it is fair to pay £100 for 3 courses. It may, however, look at other things, such as the rights of the company and the individual to cancel the lunch, and when the price is due to be paid.

Section 65: Bar on exclusion or restriction of negligence liability and Section 66: Scope of section 65

318. Section 65 provides that a trader cannot, in a consumer contract or consumer notice, limit liability for death or personal injury resulting from negligence.

319. With regard to other loss or damage (such as death or personal injury not resulting from negligence), the trader can only limit its liability if the clause is 'fair'. Whether a term is fair is determined by the fairness test, set out in section 62.

320. For example, if an individual contracts with a catering company to provide a buffet lunch, and a term in that contract states that the catering company accepts no responsibility for death by food poisoning caused by their negligence, that term is not binding. The catering company can, however, and providing the clause is fair, limit liability if it breaks kitchen equipment.

321. This bar does not apply to a discharge or indemnity given as part of a compensation settlement. This allows parties to settle disputes which have arisen concerning the performance of an earlier contract. Section 66 expressly provides that this bar does not apply to agreements mentioned in section 4(2)(a) of the Damages (Scotland) Act 2011, because not all agreements to discharge liability will include compensation.

322. Section 65 does not affect section 5 of the Damages (Scotland) Act 2011, which sets out special rules for settlement of mesothelioma claims in Scotland, and provides that relatives can still claim certain damages in some cases even if the original liability were discharged.

323. In some cases, under common law, if an individual is aware of a risk, but ignores it, he/she may be deemed to have taken on that risk. However, this provision explains that, in contrast, a consumer cannot be assumed to have taken on any risk by agreeing to a term which limits a trader's liability.

324. Terms which are barred under this section are still assessable for fairness under section 62.

325. This section reflects section 2 (for England, Wales and Northern Ireland) and section 16 (for Scotland) of the UCTA.

Section 67: Effect of an unfair term on the rest of a contract

326. As explained above, a court can find a particular term to be unfair, rendering it unenforceable. However, it may not be in the interests of the consumer or the business for the entire contract not to be binding any more. Therefore, in so far as is practical, the contract will continue even if one or more terms within it are deemed unfair.

327. This section reflects regulation 6(1) of the UTCCD, which is implemented by Article 8(2) of the UTCCRs.

*Section 68: **Requirement for transparency***

328. Whilst previous sections explain that a term in a consumer contract or a consumer notice must be fair, and how that is determined, this section states that, in addition, written terms and written notices must be transparent (defined as legible and in plain and intelligible language). The trader has an obligation to ensure that such terms are transparent.

329. This requirement, like others in this Act, may be enforced by public bodies under the relevant provisions, including under Part 8 of the EA, if the conditions in that Act are met (for example, if the term harms the collective interest of consumers). It may also be enforced under Schedule 3.

330. This section reflects regulation 7(1) of the UTCCRs, which implements Article 5 of the UTCCD.

*Section 69: **Contract terms that may have different meanings***

331. Contract terms can be ambiguous and capable of being interpreted in different ways, especially if they are not in writing or in an accessible format. In these cases, this section ensures that the interpretation that is most beneficial to the consumer, rather than the trader, is the interpretation that is used.

332. This section reflects regulation 7(2) of the UTCCRs, which implements Article 5 of the UTCCD.

How are the general rules enforced?

*Section 70: **Enforcement of the law on unfair contract terms***

333. If traders do use (or propose to use or recommend the use of) unfair, void and/or non-transparent terms in consumer contracts or consumer notices, there are a number of means of enforcing this Part.

334. This section introduces Schedule 3 which sets out how this Part can be enforced. Schedule 3 explains that the Competition and Markets Authority ("CMA") and other Regulators (coordinated by the CMA) can investigate and apply for injunctions to prevent the use of certain terms. These are terms which the CMA or other Regulator considers might be unfair, not transparent or void (for example if they purport to exclude liability for death or personal injury through negligence). The CMA or other Regulator may take action if it thinks that a term or notice falls into one or more of those three categories.

335. Schedule 3 includes provisions for the CMA to collate and if appropriate make public information about actions taken against certain terms and notices. It also provides that the CMA may issue guidance if it considers it appropriate to do so.

336. There are other means of enforcement available, for example private action by the consumer through the courts or enforcement by a public body through Part 8 of the EA.

337. Schedule 5 also includes one additional power made available to Unfair Terms enforcers. This is the power to require the production of information (Part 3 of Schedule 5). As set out in paragraph 6 of Schedule 5, this power is only available to those enforcers listed in Schedule 3 which are also public authorities (within the meaning of the Human Rights Act 1998). So, for example, this power is not available to the Consumers' Association (known as Which?).

338. This section reflects regulations 10 to 15 of the UTCCRs, which implement Article 7 of the UTCCD.

Supplementary provisions

Section 71: Duty of court to consider fairness of term

339. Courts hear a wide variety of disputes between traders and consumers concerning contracts. However, courts are not always specifically asked to look at the fairness of a term in a consumer contract. This provision places a duty upon the courts to look at the fairness of terms even if the parties do not specifically ask the court to do so.

340. This section reflects the view of the EUCJ in Case C-168/05 *Mostaza Claro* (2006) ECR I-10421 that "the nature and importance of the public interest underlying the protection which the Directive confers on consumers justify, moreover, the national court being required to assess of its own motion whether a contractual term is unfair" (paragraph 38).

341. In fulfilling this duty, the courts would not have to look at the fairness of the term if they do not have adequate information to do so, as was emphasised by the Court of Justice in Case C-243/08 *Pannon* (2009) ECR I-4713 (at para.35). In addition, the courts would only have to look at the term or terms in question, not the entire contract; this reflects the principle in Case C-137/08 *VB Penzugyi v Schneider* in 2010.

Section 72: Application of rules to secondary contracts

342. This section clarifies that the requirement for terms to be fair, as set out above, extends to contracts agreed in addition to the original contract, whether or not they are contracts between a trader and a consumer. This provides additional protection for consumers, by ensuring that any agreements made after, before or in addition to the signing of a contract are also covered by these rules.

Section 73: Disapplication of rules to mandatory terms and notices

343. This section ensures that the new and amended provisions on unfair terms do not override legal requirements in other legislation. This may be relevant, for example, where several pieces of legislation affect a trader's business.

344. This section reflects regulation 4(2) of the UTCCRs, which implements Article 1(2) of the UTCCD.

Section 74: Contracts applying law of non-EEA State

345. The parties to a contract may agree that it is to be governed by the law of a particular country. This might be because the trader is based in a country other than the UK. This section provides that the consumer may not be deprived of the protection of this Part, where a contract has a close connection with the UK, even if the contract states that the law of a non-EEA State applies (the EEA is the EU Member States plus Iceland, Liechtenstein and Norway).

346. The Rome I Regulation (Regulation (EC) No 593/2008 of the European Parliament and of the Council of 17 June 2008 on the law applicable to contractual obligations)[35], governs which law applies to a consumer contract. See paragraph 27 above for more information on the Rome I Regulation.

347. Section 74 is based on regulation 9 of the UTCCRs, which implements Article 6(2) of the UTCCD; and sections 26 and 27 of the UCTA.

---

35 For contracts entered into before 17 December 2009, the Rome Convention applies (Convention 80/934/ECC on the law applicable to contractual obligations opened for signature in Rome on 19 June 1980).

Section 75: Changes to other legislation

348. This section gives effect to Schedule 4 which lists amendments required to other legislation, including the UCTA, as a result of this Part.

Part 3 Miscellaneous and General

Chapter 1: Enforcement Etc.

Section 77: Investigatory powers etc.

349. This section makes provision for the investigatory powers of consumer law enforcers. Consumer law, which includes enforcers' investigatory powers, has built up piecemeal, resulting in the investigatory powers, contained in around 60 pieces of consumer legislation, being unclear, inconsistent and overlapping each other. In its consultation published in March 2012 entitled 'Enhancing Consumer Confidence Through Effective Enforcement – Consultation on consolidating and modernising consumer law enforcement powers,' BIS proposed simplifying the powers by consolidating them into one generic set.

350. This section gives effect to Schedule 5 on Investigatory Powers and Schedule 6 which details the consequential amendments in relation to the investigatory powers.

Schedule 5: Investigatory Powers etc.

351. This Schedule contains a generic set of powers, which is based on those currently contained in Part 4 of the Consumer Protection from Unfair Trading Regulations 2008 (CPRs). This is because CPRs are relatively modern; reflect current business practices; build on similar existing legislation and can be used to investigate breaches which may lead to criminal or civil proceedings. Some specific powers contained in weights and measures and product safety legislation will be retained in that legislation alongside the generic set.

352. As well as consolidating powers that already exist, stronger safeguards have been added to the use of some powers in order to reduce the burdens on businesses. For example, subject to a number of exemptions, the power of entry into premises without a warrant cannot be exercised unless a notice in writing has been given to the occupier at least two working days before an inspection is carried out and the power exercised. This requirement applies to routine inspections only and the Schedule sets out those circumstances that would not amount to a routine inspection.

353. As a consequence of consolidating these powers, some modification has been necessary to the existing powers, either to ensure compliance with EU obligations, or to align powers across consumer law in order to ensure that the powers contained in the generic set are simple and consistent. For example, the generic set includes a power to require production of information under paragraph 14 of Part 3 of the Schedule, which is based on Part 8 of the EA dealing with civil enforcement but which will now apply to both civil and criminal consumer law enforcement.

354. In some instances, a limitation has been specifically placed on the use of a particular power. For example, the power to require production of information can only be used if the enforcer reasonably suspects a breach of legislation. This limitation does not apply, or apply in the same way, for all types of enforcer.

355. The generic set of powers applies to all enforcers detailed in the Schedule except where access to powers is specifically limited for particular enforcers. For example, the powers of unfair contract terms enforcers and public designated enforcers, are restricted to the power to require production of information.

356. Paragraph 1 of Part 1 provides an overview of the Parts of Schedule 5.

357. Paragraphs 2 to 6 detail the types of enforcers that have access to the powers in the Schedule and define the terms used to refer to those enforcers, *e.g.* EU and domestic enforcers. Paragraph 7 details what is meant by the term 'officer' in relation to enforcers whilst Paragraph 8 defines other terms used in the Schedule.

358. Paragraphs 9 to 11 of Part 2 of the Schedule specify the legislation to which the generic set of powers applies.

359. Paragraph 12 introduces a power for the Secretary of State by order to amend the list of legislation to which the generic set of powers applies. This is to ensure that the generic set of powers can be used to enforce any new duties that may in future be prescribed.

360. The order making power would also allow other legislation to be amended, repealed or revoked as a consequence of amending this list. The safeguards on the use of the powers of entry that replace those being repealed must be greater than those that existed before.

361. Paragraphs 13 to 17 of Part 3 of the Schedule detail the power in relation to the production of information. These paragraphs set out the purposes for which the power can be used, the procedure to be followed when using it and how the power can be enforced, as well as limitations on the use of the information obtained.

362. Paragraph 18 clarifies that Part 3 of the Schedule applies to the Crown to the same extent that the relevant powers in Part 8 of the EA (which are being replaced by the powers in the Schedule) applied to the Crown.

363. Paragraph 19 to 20 of Part 4 of the Schedule sets out the purposes for which the further powers in the generic set detailed in this Part may be exercised by domestic and EU enforcers. These further powers are detailed in paragraphs 21 to 34. Table 1 and Table 2 below summarises how the powers in the generic set have been modified compared to those in the CPRs and other relevant legislation. The new safeguards that have been added are highlighted in bold.

364. These provisions in the Act give effect in part to certain EU legislation by providing domestic regulators with the necessary powers for enforcing such legislation. This includes the Regulation on Consumer Protection Cooperation[36], the Regulation on Accreditation and Market Surveillance[37] and the General Product Safety Directive[38].

365. The existing investigatory powers are being repealed or revoked in order to ensure that only the generic set of powers apply in relation to the consumer legislation within the scope of this Schedule.

TABLE 1: SUMMARY OF MAIN MODIFICATIONS FROM EXISTING INVESTIGATIVE POWERS IN THE NEW GENERIC SET IN PART 3 OF SCHEDULE 5 (NEW SAFEGUARDS ARE HIGHLIGHTED IN BOLD)

Power/Provision	***Modelled on***	***Main modifications from existing provisions***
Paragraphs 13 to 17 – Power to require production of information (by way of a written notice only)	Section 224 to 227 EA	Certain enforcers, such as unfair contract terms enforcers and public designated enforcers, have access to this power only.
		Some enforcers are required to reasonably suspect a breach before exercising the power.
		Clarifies that it includes a power to require the creation of documents.

36 (EC) No 2006/2004.
37 (EC) No 765/2008.
38 2001/95/EC.

Power/Provision	*Modelled on*	*Main modifications from existing provisions*
		Clarifies that local weights and measures authorities have access to this power specifically for the purposes of fulfilling duties conferred by the Estate Agents Act 1979.
		Can be used for both criminal and civil enforcement purposes.
		Provision is made regarding protection from self-incrimination.
Paragraph 18 Application to the Crown		Clarifies that Part 3 of the Schedule applies to the Crown when an enforcer is acting for certain purposes.

TABLE 2: SUMMARY OF MAIN MODIFICATIONS FROM EXISTING INVESTIGATIVE POWERS IN THE NEW GENERIC SET IN PART 4 OF SCHEDULE 5 (NEW SAFEGUARDS ARE HIGHLIGHTED IN BOLD)

Power/Provision	*Modelled on*	*Main modifications from existing provisions*
Paragraph 19 – Exercise of powers in this Part: Domestic enforcers	Regulation 21(1) CPRs and section 9 Estate Agents Act 1979	Details the purposes and circumstances in which the powers in this Part can be exercised by domestic enforcers.
		Clarifies that for the power to require production of documents, the enforcer need not have reasonable suspicion where there is a statutory duty to hold the documents sought or when the enforcer is a market surveillance authority as defined by the Regulation on Accreditation and Market Surveillance (EC 765/2008).
		Clarifies that the powers can be used to investigate undesirable practices under Estate Agents Act 1979 as well as breaches of it.
Paragraph 20 - Exercise of powers in this Part: EU Enforcers		Details the purposes and circumstances in which the powers in this Part can be exercised by EU enforcers.
Paragraph 21 – Power to purchase products	Regulation 20 CPRs	A new express provision is added to clarify that enforcers may enter premises normally open to the public and inspect products.
		The definition of officer in paragraph 7(1)(d) extends this power to authorised persons (*e.g.* volunteers).Clarification that power may be exercised at all reasonable times.
		Clarification that this power can be exercised without first giving notice or obtaining a warrant.

Power/Provision	***Modelled on***	***Main modifications from existing provisions***
Paragraph 22 – Power to observe the carrying on of a business	Section 227B(1)(a) EA	A new express provision is added to clarify that enforcers may enter premises accessible to the public to observe businesses.
		Clarification that the power may be exercised at all reasonable times.
		Clarification that this power can be exercised without first giving notice or obtaining a warrant.
Paragraph 23 – Power to enter premises without warrant	Regulation 21(1)(a) CPRs (Currently excludes premises used only as a dwelling)	The power excludes entry to premises which are wholly or **mainly** private dwellings.
		In relation to routine inspections there is a requirement to give written notice. There must be two working days between the date of receipt of the notice by the occupier and the date of entry by the enforcer. A routine inspection is defined in Schedule 5 as one where none of the circumstances in sub-paragraph (6) apply. These include circumstances where notice would defeat the purpose of the entry, *e.g.* because an officer reasonably suspects that evidence may be lost or destroyed if notice is given, such as where counterfeit goods are suspected. Notice also need not be given where the occupier has waived the requirement.
		If advance notice is not given, enforcers are required to give notice to occupiers when entering the premises.
		Enforcers are required to provide evidence of their authorisation and identity, whether or not advance notice has been given.
		Clarification that proceedings are not invalid where there is a failure to provide notice or evidence of authorisation.
Paragraph 24 – Application of paragraphs 25 to 31		Clarifies that the powers in paragraphs 25 – 31 are only exercisable when the enforcer has entered premises under paragraph 23(1) or under a warrant under paragraph 32 - 33.
Paragraph 25 – Power to inspect products etc.	Regulation 21(1)(a) CPRs	This includes the power to inspect products, records and to examine any procedure on the premises, as well as inspecting any apparatus or fixed installation as defined in Electromagnetic Compatibility Regulations 2006 (SI 2006/3418).

Power/Provision	***Modelled on***	***Main modifications from existing provisions***
Paragraph 26 – Power to test equipment	Weights and Measures Act 1985 and Weights and Measures (Packaged Goods) Regulations 2006	This power enables enforcers to test weighing and measuring instruments on the premises.
Paragraphs 27 – Power to require production of documents	Regulation 21(1)(b) CPRs	Clarifies that this power includes requiring an explanation of documents.
		Clarification that the power does not permit an officer to require a person to create a document except where documents are held electronically.
		Clarification that the power can be applied to a business under investigation or another person.
Paragraph 28 – Power to seize and detain goods	Regulation 21(c) CPRs	**Requirement for enforcers to provide evidence of their authorisation and identity, whether or not it is requested by the occupier, unless it is impractical to do so.**
		Requirement to issue a written record of goods seized.
		The power is available where an enforcer reasonably suspects goods may disclose a breach of legislation; that goods are liable to be forfeited or that they may be required as evidence in proceedings.
		The time limit on detention for goods is three months, unless they are reasonably needed for longer, *e.g.* for use in proceedings.
		Requirement for certain enforcers to have regard to any relevant provision on property seizure in a code of practice under section 66 Police and Criminal Evidence Act 1984 or Article 65Police and Criminal Evidence (Northern Ireland) Order 1989 (SI 1989/1341 (NI 12)).
Paragraph 29 – Power to seize and detain documents required as evidence	Regulation 21(d) CPRs	**Requirement for enforcers to provide evidence of their authorisation and identity, whether or not it is requested by the occupier, unless it is impractical to do so.**
		Requirement to issue a written record of documents seized.

Power/Provision	***Modelled on***	***Main modifications from existing provisions***
		The power is available where an enforcer reasonably suspects they may be required as evidence in proceedings.
		The time limit on detention for documents is three months, unless they are reasonably needed for longer for use in proceedings.
		Requirement for certain enforcers to have regard to any relevant provision on property seizure in a code of practice under section 66 Police and Criminal Evidence Act 1984 or Article 65Police and Criminal Evidence (Northern Ireland) Order 1989 (SI 1989/1341 (NI 12)).
Paragraph 30 – Power to decommission or switch off fixed installations	Regulation 37 Electromagnetic Compatibility Regulations 2006	Confers a power to decommission or switch off fixed installations (as defined in the Electromagnetic Compatibility Regulations 2006).
Paragraph 31 – Power to break open a container/vending machine	Regulation 21(2) CPRs	Clarification that the power includes access to information held on electronic devices, such as computers including those on a network.
		Clarification on what constitutes a container.
Paragraphs 32 to 33 – Power to enter premises with a warrant	Combination of Regulation 22 CPRs and 227C EA	Includes a condition that a Justice of the Peace must be satisfied that certain conditions have been met, such as that it is likely that goods or documents may be concealed or interfered with, if notice of entry were given.
		Where premises are unoccupied or occupier is temporally absent, officers will be required to issue a notice on leaving the premises stating that the premises have been entered under warrant and to leave the premises secured as found.
Paragraph 34 – Power to require assistance from persons on the premises	Provision under Weights and Measures legislation	Requirement for persons on premises to provide assistance or information reasonably required by the officer.
		Clarification that the power includes requiring a person on the premises to provide information about the name and address of the packer or importer of a package which the officer finds on the premises.

366. Additionally, Part 5 of the Schedule provides supplementary provisions. Paragraphs 36 and 37 respectively designate the acts of obstructing officers of enforcers and purporting

to act as such an officer when not so authorised as offences. These and other provisions in the generic set are detailed in Table 3 below.

TABLE 3: SUPPLEMENTARY PROVISIONS IN PART 5 OF SCHEDULE 5 (NEW SAFEGUARDS ARE HIGHLIGHTED IN BOLD)

Provision	***Modelled on***	***Main modifications from existing provisions in CPRs***
Paragraph 36 - Offence of obstruction	Combination of Regulation 23 CPRs and regulation 24(2)(b) General Product Safety Regulations 2005	Clarification that this offence applies in relation to powers exercised under Part 4.
		Includes an offence of recklessly making a statement which is false. Maximum penalties are aligned at level 3 on the standard scale.
		Clarification that a person commits an offence if they give misleading information.
Paragraph 37 - Offence of purporting to act as officer	Regulation 21(11) CPRs	Clarification that the level of the maximum penalty for this offence may be subject to amendment by section 85 of the Legal Aid, Sentencing and Punishment of Offenders Act 2012 and regulations made under that provision.
Paragraph 38 - Access to seized goods and documents		**Enforcers must grant reasonable access to goods and documents seized, *e.g.* so that copies of seized documents can be made. Enforcers may recover the reasonable costs of complying with such a request.**
Paragraph 39 - Notice of testing goods	Combination of Regulation 24 CPRs and Consumer Protection Act 1987 (CPA) and Electromagnetic Compatibility Regulations 2006	Clarification that there is a requirement for notice also to be given where the test leads to issuing of a suspension notice or the forfeiture of the goods.
Paragraph 40 - Appeals against detention of goods	Section 33 CPA	None.
Paragraph 41 – Compensation	Regulation 25 CPRs	None.

367. Also in Part 6 of this Schedule, the law in relation to the ability of Trading Standards Services is clarified to ensure that they are able to operate across local authority boundaries efficiently and effectively. This is set out at paragraphs 44 to 46 of the Schedule.

Section 78: Amendment of the Weights and Measures (Packaged Goods) Regulations 2006

368. This section provides an automatic exemption from keeping records of checks for packers of bread which is sold unwrapped or in open packs.

Section 79: Enterprise Act 2002: enhanced consumer measures and other enforcement

Introduction

369. The intention of this part of the Act is to amend Part 8 of the EA to allow the courts to attach a range of enhanced consumer measures to enforcement orders and undertakings. Public enforcers will also be able to agree undertakings under Part 8 that include enhanced consumer measures.

370. The main aim of the section is to give the civil courts and public enforcers flexibility when dealing with persons who have given undertakings or who are subject to enforcement orders. The section will allow a range of enhanced consumer measures that are just, reasonable and proportionate, to be attached to enforcement orders and undertakings.

371. The section will also introduce a power for the Secretary of State to extend the use of the enhanced consumer measures to private designated enforcers.

Background

372. When there is a breach or potential breach of consumer law, the measures available to public enforcers are limited and there is a lack of flexibility in the ways that they can achieve better outcomes for consumers and compliant businesses. The main formal sanction is a criminal prosecution of the trader by an enforcer. While this can benefit consumers as it prevents the spread of instances of illegal trading, in practice there is generally no direct remedy for victims of the breach.

373. As an alternative to criminal prosecution, certain enforcers can seek civil injunctive relief under Part 8 of the EA against infringements of consumer protection legislation. The key mechanism is an enforcement order. Through an enforcement order, a civil court can order that the infringer stop engaging in the conduct in question. It can also order that the infringer publish the enforcement order and a corrective statement, aiming to eliminate the continued effect of an infringement. Alternatively, a court or an enforcer may accept an undertaking from the business that they will not engage in conduct that involves an infringement. However, civil enforcement will not generally give remedies to individual consumers or secure positive action by businesses.

374. The Government's response[39] to the consultation 'Extending the Range of Remedies Available to Public Enforcers of Consumer Law'[40] sets out further information on the measures in this section. The response also confirms the Government's intention that the new enhanced consumer measures should always be just, reasonable and proportionate and aimed at achieving one or more of the following:

- redress for consumers who have suffered loss from breaches of consumer law;
- improved compliance and a reduction in the likelihood of future breaches; and
- more information being provided to consumers so they can exercise greater choice and in doing so improve the functioning of the market for consumers and businesses generally.

---

39 https://www.gov.uk/government/uploads/system/uploads/attachment_data/file/206373/bis-13-916-draft-consumer-rights-bill-governemnt-response-to-consultations-on-consumer-rights.pdf

40 www.bis.gov.uk/Consultations/consultation-rationalising-modernising-consumer-law?cat=closedawaitingresponse Consultation on extending the range of remedies available to public enforcers of consumer law

375. Details of possible measures are not included in the legislation as this may risk taking away flexibility from the courts and enforcers of consumer law to identify the most suitable measure or measures to deal with a person subject to enforcement orders or undertakings. It may also take away the flexibility for a person who is subject to enforcement orders or undertakings to put forward their own measures, which could be deemed suitable, to the court or enforcer of consumer law.

Part 8 Enterprise Act 2002

376. Part 8 of the EA enables certain enforcers to take civil action in respect of infringements of specified domestic/Community consumer legislation which harm the collective interests of consumers.

377. The enforcement procedure is set out at sections 214 to 223 of the EA. Key to this procedure is an application for an enforcement order (under section 215), following consultation with the business and notification of the CMA[41], which can then be issued by the court (under section 217). As an alternative to issuing an enforcement order, the court may accept undertakings (section 217(9)). Similarly, as an alternative to making an application for an enforcement order the enforcer may accept undertakings (section 219).

Enforcers

378. There are a number of enforcers who are able to use this enforcement procedure. Some enforcers are specialist, within a particular market, for example the CAA; whereas others, like Trading Standards Services have a broader remit. The EA (section 213) provides for the following categories of enforcer: general[42]; designated[43]; community[44]; and CPC[45].

379. Under section 213(4), the Secretary of State may designate a person or body which is not a public body only if the person or body (as the case may be) satisfies such criteria as the Secretary of State specifies by Order. Currently only the Consumers' Association (Which?) is designated as such.

380. The new enhanced consumer measures will only be available where the enforcer is a public body. A power is included to extend the use of the measures to private designated enforcers if certain conditions are met.

381. The section amends Part 8 of the EA to enable enforcement orders or undertakings to include new enhanced consumer measures, in addition to requirements that could be made under the existing legislation (i.e. generally a requirement to stop, or to not engage in the conduct that constitutes a breach of consumer law).

382. Section 79 introduces Schedule 7 and limits the use of the enhanced consumer measures to breaches or potential breaches of consumer law that occur, or are likely to occur, after the commencement of this section.

---

41 Section 214 was amended by Article 9 of SI 2013/783.

42 Competition and Markets Authority, Trading Standards Services in Great Britain; Department of Enterprise, Trade and Investment in Northern Ireland.

43 Designated, see SI 2003/1399 as amended SI 2005/917 and SI 2013/478: the Civil Aviation Authority, the Northern Ireland Authority for Utility Regulation, Ofcom, the Water Services Regulation Authority, the Gas and Electricity Markets Authority, the Information Commissioner, the Office of Rail Regulation, the Consumers' Association and the Financial Conduct Authority.

44 A qualified entity for the purposes of the Injunctions Directive EC 98/27 (Injunctions for the protection of consumers' interests) which is specified in the list published in the Official Journal of the European Community, but is not a general, designated or CPC enforcer.

45 Competition and Markets Authority, Civil Aviation Authority, Financial Conduct Authority, Secretary of State for Health, Department of Health Social Services and Public Safety in Northern Ireland, Ofcom, Department of Enterprise, Trade and Investment in Northern Ireland, every local weights and measures authority, Independent Committee for the Supervision of Standards of the Telephone Information Services, the Information Commissioner.

Schedule 7: Enterprise Act 2002: enhanced consumer measures and other enforcement

383. The aim of Schedule 7 is to provide greater flexibility for public enforcers and the civil courts in relation to the contents of enforcement orders and undertakings made under Part 8 of the EA. If they are deemed suitable for a particular case, public enforcers and the civil courts will be able to attach (where they consider it just and reasonable) enhanced consumer measures to enforcement orders and undertakings. The enhanced consumer measures will need to fall into at least one of three specified categories (referred to as the redress, compliance and choice categories). Measures in the redress category will offer compensation or other redress to consumers who have suffered loss as a result of the breach of consumer law. Compliance measures are intended to increase business compliance with the law and to reduce the likelihood of further breaches. Measures in the choice category will help consumers obtain relevant market information to enable them to make better purchasing decisions.

384. Paragraphs 2 and 3 amend sections 210 and 211 of the EA to widen the injunctive regime under Part 8. This will enable enforcers to use it for infringements of domestic legislation that harm the collective interests of consumers where either the supplier or the consumer is in the UK.

385. Paragraph 4 updates the list of enforcers in the EA.

386. Paragraph 5 amends section 214 (consultation), and sub-paragraph (2) extends from 14 to 28 days the consultation period for enforcers of consumer law before they can take action against a person for an enforcement order or undertaking in cases where the new subsection (4A) applies (see paragraph 389 below).

387. Sub paragraph (3) inserts a new subsection (4A) that describes when the extended 28 day period applies. It applies in those cases where the person that may be subjected to the enforcement order or undertaking is a member of, or represented by, a trade association or other business representative body that operates a consumer code of practice that has been approved by a public enforcement body or a community interest company whose role includes the approval of consumer codes.

388. In practice, the extended consultation period may be used, for example, by the person that may be subject to the enforcement order or undertaking to propose their own measures which may include addressing the detriment caused and be based on the requirements of the relevant consumer code. Depending on the circumstances of the case, this may be an indicator that the infringement will not be repeated. At the end of the 28 day period, the enforcer of consumer law may take further action if they consider it appropriate. They can either commence court action to seek an enforcement order and/or seek to work with the person to agree undertakings.

389. Paragraph 6 amends section 217 (enforcement orders) inserting new subsections (10A) to (10D). New subsection (10A) provides a power for the court to attach enhanced consumer measures defined in section 219A (paragraph 395 below) to an enforcement order and for the court to specify an appropriate time period for the person to comply with the enhanced consumer measures.

390. New subsection (10B) allows the court to attach enhanced consumer measures to an undertaking accepted under section (9) and for the court to specify an appropriate time period for the person to comply with the enhanced consumer measures.

391. New subsection (10C) restricts the court from attaching enhanced consumer measures to an enforcement order or undertaking sought by a private enforcer unless the conditions in new section 219C are met.

392. New subsection (10D) allows the court to include in an enforcement order or undertaking a requirement that the person subject to the enforcement order or

undertaking provide information or documentation to the court to show that they have complied with the enhanced consumer measures.

393. Paragraph 7 amends section 219 (undertakings) inserting new subsections (5ZA) and (5ZB). New subsection (5ZA) enables public enforcers to include enhanced consumer measures in undertakings and to be provided with documentation from the person subject to the undertaking and to specify an appropriate time period for the person to comply with the enhanced consumer measures. Subsection (5ZA) also requires the person subject to the undertaking to provide information or documents to the enforcer to enable them to determine if the person is carrying out the enhanced consumer measures agreed in the undertaking.

394. New subsection (5ZB) restricts private enforcers from agreeing an undertaking with enhanced consumer measures unless the conditions in new section 219C are met.

395. Paragraph 8 inserts new sections 219A (definition of enhanced consumer measures) and 219B (inclusion of enhanced consumer measures etc) and 219C (availability of enhanced consumer measures to private enforcers). New section 219A(1) lists the three categories of enhanced consumer measures – redress, compliance and choice. Subsections (2) to (5) describe those measures.

396. New subsection (2) describes the first category of measures - the redress category. New subsection (2)(a) limits compensation or redress to those consumers who have suffered loss as a result of the breach of consumer law. This is mirrored in new section 219B(4)(a). Consumers retain the right to refuse offers of redress, whether in an enforcement order or undertaking, and instead take their own civil action against the person that has caused them detriment. Where the infringing conduct relates to a contract, new subsection (2)(b) states that measures in the redress category can include giving consumers the option to terminate that contract. New subsection (2)(c) allows for measures intended to be in the collective interests of consumers in cases where consumers who have suffered detriment cannot be identified or it would require a disproportionate cost to do so. Measures in these circumstances could include, for example, the non-compliant business making a charitable donation equivalent to the value of the detriment caused to consumers (where that charity acts in the interests of consumers). New subsection (2)(c) only applies in the circumstances outlined above. It does not apply in circumstances where consumers who have been identified as suffering detriment choose to decline the redress offered.

397. New subsections (3) and (4) describe the measures in the second and third categories – the compliance and choice categories. Measures in these categories might include the person subject to the enforcement order or undertaking:

- appointing a compliance officer;
- introducing a complaints handling process;
- improving their record keeping;
- signing up to an established customer review / feedback site; or
- publicising details of the breach or potential breach, and what they have done to put the situation right in the local or national press or on social media.

398. New subsection (5) excludes the existing publication requirements within Part 8 of the EA from the scope of the new enhanced consumer measures.

399. New section 219B sets out the requirements that apply to the inclusion of enhanced consumer measures within an enforcement order or undertaking. New subsection (1) confirms that only just and reasonable enhanced consumer measures can be attached to enforcement orders or undertakings under this Part. New subsections (2) and (3) set out the factors the court or enforcer must take into account. This includes a specific

requirement that the measures must be proportionate, taking into account the costs of the measures (to business and consumers) and the benefit to consumers.

400. New subsections (4) to (5) make provision in relation to a loss case (which is defined in new subsections (9) and (10)). These provisions restrict the imposition of enhanced consumer measures in the redress category to cases where there has been a loss suffered by consumers and require that in those cases, the court or enforcer must be satisfied that the cost to the person subject to the enforcement order or undertaking of complying with the measures is unlikely to exceed the loss suffered by consumers. However, the administrative costs (i.e. the cost of setting up and running the redress scheme) should not be included in this calculation.

401. New subsections (6) and (7) limit any waiver sought by the person who is subject to an enforcement order or undertaking, from consumers as part of a compensation scheme, so that the waiver is not valid to the extent that it seeks to cover conduct which is not covered by the enforcement order or undertaking. For example, the waiver will not be valid if it relates to additional goods or services that were not covered by the enforcement order or undertaking.

402. New section 219C sets out the conditions that must be met before enhanced consumer measures can be sought in an undertaking or order sought by a private enforcer.

403. New subsection (3) sets out the first condition, which is that the enforcer must have been specified by the Secretary of State in an Order under this section.

404. New subsection (4) sets out the second condition, which is that the enhanced consumer measures must not directly benefit the enforcer or an associated undertaking. New subsection (5) sets out particular types of measure that would be considered as directly benefitting the enforcer or an associated undertaking. These include requiring a person to pay money to the private enforcer, requiring a person to participate in a scheme designed to recommend goods or services that is administered by the private enforcer or where the measure would give the private enforcer a commercial advantage over any of its competitors.

405. New subsection (6) provides that the Secretary of State can only exercise the power in subsection (3) to extend the use of the enhanced consumer measures to a private enforcer if they are satisfied that it will result in:

- more redress being paid to consumers;
- more information being provided to consumers to enable them to make better informed purchasing decisions; and/or
- more compliance by business with the law.

406. New subsection (7) provides that the Secretary of State can only use the power in subsection (3) if the private enforcer is subject to the principles of good regulation in the Regulators Code and section 21 of the Legislative and Regulatory Reform Act 2006 (transparency, accountability, proportionality, consistency and targeting cases that need action).

407. New subsections (9) and (10) set out a requirement on private enforcers that when using enhanced consumer measures they must act consistently with advice or guidance given by a primary authority.

408. New subsection (11) defines "associated undertaking".

409. Paragraph 9 makes amendments to section 220 of the EA (further proceedings), which makes provision for further applications to the court where there has been a failure to comply with an enforcement order or undertaking made under sections 217 and 218 of the EA. Sub-paragraph (2) inserts a new subsection (1A) which provides that

section 220 does not apply where the only failure is a failure to comply with the information requirement in new subsection 217(10D).

410. Subsection 220(2) of the EA gives the CMA the same right to apply to the court in respect of a failure to comply with an order or undertaking as the enforcer that made the application for the order. Sub-paragraph (3) amends subsection 220(2) to provide that any CPC enforcer (defined in section 213(5A)) has that right, not just the CMA.

411. Sub-paragraph (4) contains related or consequential amendments to Part 8 of the EA.

412. Paragraph 10 updates the EA to reflect the enforcement of Schedule 5 in the Consumer Rights Act 2015.

*Section 80: **Contravention of code regulating premium rate services***

413. Under sections 120 to 123 of the Communications Act 2003, providers of premium rate services are obliged to comply with the code published by the regulator, PhonepayPlus, and approved by Ofcom for the purposes of regulating such services. Premium rate services are a form of micro-payment for content, data services and value added services charged to a telephone bill. They include services such as directory inquiries, voting in competitions and quizzes, business information lines, making charity donations by text and making payment for digital goods and services.

414. PhonepayPlus may impose a maximum penalty of £250,000 in respect of a contravention of the code. For example, some providers may use intentionally misleading promotional material or fail to provide clear pricing information, leaving consumers out of pocket.

415. This section amends these provisions to make clear that the maximum penalty of £250,000 can be imposed in respect of each breach of the code and not, as has been argued by some providers, just once regardless of the number of provisions of the code that have been breached in any one set of proceedings against a provider.

416. This will allow PhonepayPlus to impose penalties of more than £250,000 in appropriate cases and where it is proportionate to do so.

*Chapter 2: **Competition***

Summary and Background

417. This Chapter deals with the scope and operation of the Competition Appeals Tribunal. It introduces provisions to make it easier for consumers and businesses to gain access to redress where there has been an infringement of antitrust provisions ("competition law"), and addresses the unintended barriers in the current process to the appointment of Scottish and Northern Irish judges to sit as chairmen in the Competition Appeal Tribunal (CAT).

*Section 81: **Private actions in competition law***

418. Section 81 and Schedule 8 have three main aims:

- To widen the types of the competition cases that the Competition Appeal Tribunal hears ("CAT") (see paragraph 420 to 433 below) and to make other changes to the procedure of bringing a private action before the CAT;
- To provide for opt-out collective actions and opt-out collective settlements (see paragraphs 434 to 445 below);
- To provide for voluntary redress schemes (see paragraph 446 to 450 below).

419. The Government's response to the consultation "Private Actions in Competition Law"[46], explains the proposals for reform of claims for damages under the private actions framework in Part 3 of this Act. There are also further proposed changes accompanying these sections in the CAT's rules which govern how it deals with cases.

Widen the types of cases which the CAT can hear

420. The CAT is a specialist tribunal whose function is to hear cases involving competition issues. However, at present, the CAT is restricted in which competition law cases it can consider. The CAT is able to hear follow-on cases. A follow-on action is brought after an infringement has been found by "a relevant competition authority", which are the Competition and Markets Authority ("CMA"), European Commission and the following relevant sector regulators with competition powers:

- The Office of Gas and Electricity Markets ("Ofgem");
- The Office of Communications ("Ofcom");
- The Water Service Regulation Authority ("Ofwat");
- Civil Aviation Authority ("CAA");
- Office of the Rail Regulator ("ORR");
- Northern Ireland Authority for Utility Regulation ("NIAUR");
- Monitor.

421. In contrast, a stand-alone claim requires the party which brings the action to prove an infringement. In *Enron v EWS* (I),[47] the Court of Appeal ruled that the scope for the CAT to go beyond the findings of the initial infringement decision is extremely limited. This judgment is widely thought to be one of the contributing factors restricting the role of the CAT in competition law actions in the current regime. Businesses or consumers who wish to bring stand-alone cases must bring their case in the High Court of England and Wales, the Court of Session or the Sheriff Court in Scotland or the High Court of Northern Ireland.

422. In addition, whilst the CAT may award damages for follow-on actions, it does not have the power to grant injunctions (an order which prohibits a party from doing a particular act). This restriction prevents a party from obtaining redress from the CAT in the form of an order prohibiting, for example, anti-competitive pricing. At present, a party seeking an injunction would need to apply to the High Court.

423. Paragraph 4 replaces section 47A of the Competition Act 1998 ("CA") which currently only provides for follow-on cases to be brought before the CAT. Paragraph 4 enables the CAT to hear a stand-alone claim as well as a follow-on claim and also to have the power to grant injunctions.

424. Paragraph 31 inserts paragraph 15A of the EA to allow rules to be made providing for a fast-track procedure for claims brought under s.47A of the CA. The purpose of this is to enable simpler cases brought by small and medium enterprises ("SMEs") to be resolved more quickly and at a lower cost.

425. Paragraph 7 introduces a new section 47D of the CA, This provides that an injunction granted under s.47A and in respect of collective proceedings is enforceable as if it were granted by the High Court. This means that if the injunction is breached, a party may bring proceedings for breach of the injunction, such as contempt proceedings which could result in a penalty such as a fine.

---

46 https://www.gov.uk/government/consultations/private-actions-in-competition-law-a-consultation-on-options-for-reform
47 *English Welsh & Scottish Railway Limited v Enron Coal Services Limited* [2009] EWCA Civ 647, 1 July 2009.

426. Paragraph 24 amends Schedule 4 of the EA providing for enforcement of injunctions granted under section 47A of the CA. It does this by providing that where a party fails to comply with an injunction, the CAT may certify the matter to the High Court, i.e. sets out the facts and evidence of the matter.

427. Paragraph 34 amends Schedule 4 of EA to enable rules to be made about the grant of injunctions by the CAT.

428. Paragraph 8 introduces a new section 47E of the CA. This provides that the limitation/prescription periods (the time limit for claims to be brought) for claims before the CAT are the same as the relevant limitation/prescription period for claims before the High Court in England and Wales, the Court of Session in Scotland, the High Court in Northern Ireland. At present, the limitation period for claims before the CAT is two years, compared with six years for a claim before the High Court of England and Wales and the High Court in Northern Ireland and five years for the Court of Session in Scotland. See paragraph 442 below for how the limitation/prescription periods may be suspended in the case of collective actions.

429. Paragraph 13 amends section 58 of the CA to make clear that the CAT is bound by a finding of fact of the CMA, unless it directs otherwise. This is to ensure the CAT has sufficient flexibility when dealing with case and is in the same position as a court which hears a competition case. A court is already able to make such a direction.

430. Paragraph 9 amends section 49 of the CA to provide for a right of appeal against a decision of the CAT in proceedings brought under section 47A of the CA (stand-alone or follow-on actions) or 47B of the CA (collective proceedings). Where the appeal concerns section 47B, it may only be brought by the representative in those proceedings.

431. Paragraph 14 replaces existing section 58A of the CA. The purpose of this is to make clear when a court or the CAT is bound by a decision that there has been an infringement of competition law. This ensures the position is the same for the court and the CAT. New section 58A ensures that once an infringement decision has become final, the court or the CAT is bound by it. New section 58A sets out when a decision becomes final, for example when the time for appealing against the decision has expired without an appeal having been brought.

432. Paragraph 32 amends paragraph 17 of Schedule 4 to the EA, to enable rules to be made to enable the CAT to order payments to a legal party who has been acting on behalf of a business or consumer for free (i.e. on a pro bono basis).

433. Paragraph 33 inserts paragraph 20A of Schedule 4 to the EA which enables rules to be made which enable the CAT to stay or sist proceedings under section 47A and 47B. This is because the CAT may wish to stay (or sist) proceedings, for example if the original infringement decision is subject to appeal and that appeal has not yet been decided.

Collective actions and opt-out collective settlements

434. The second aim is to introduce an opt-out collective actions regime and an opt-out collective settlement regime (both of which involve a case being brought forward on behalf of a group of claimants to obtain compensation for their losses). Cases would be able to be brought by representatives on behalf of individuals and/or businesses.

435. The CAT can already hear opt-in collective actions under the existing section 47B of the CA. An opt-in regime requires claimants to "opt-in" to the legal action to be able to obtain any damages. However, the CAT does not currently have the power to hear opt-out collective actions. An opt-out regime means claimants are automatically included into the action unless they "opt-out" in a manner as decided by the CAT on a case by case basis. The purpose of introducing opt-out collective actions is to allow consumers and businesses to easily achieve redress for losses they have suffered as a result of breaches of competition law.

436. The function of a collective settlement regime is to introduce a procedure for infringements of competition law, where those who have suffered a loss and the alleged infringer may jointly apply to the CAT to approve the settlement of a dispute on an opt-out basis. The collective settlement regime will operate on the same opt-out principles as the opt-out collective proceedings.

437. Paragraph 5 replaces section 47B of the CA so as to provide for opt-out collective proceedings, as well as continuing to provide for opt-in collective proceedings. Subsection (11) defines opt-out collective proceedings and also provides that a person who is not domiciled in the United Kingdom must opt-in to become part of the proceedings. Subsection (10) defines opt-in collective proceedings. Subsection (4) provides that collective proceedings may only be progressed if the CAT makes a collective proceedings order. Subsection (5) provides that that CAT may only make a collective proceedings order if it considers the person who brought the proceedings meets the requirements of subsection (8) and the claims are eligible for inclusion in collective proceedings (they fall within the claims provided for in section 47A of the CA, so the proceedings may either be stand-alone or follow-on). Subsection (8) provides that a representative must be a person whom the Tribunal considers it is just and reasonable to appoint as a representative. The current section 47B of the CA only allows for named representative bodies to bring opt-in collective actions. Currently, this only includes the consumer organization Which?. The new subsection (8) will enable any appropriate representative, such as a consumer body or trade association to bring claims on behalf of consumers or businesses, as long all the claims raise the same, similar or related issues of fact or law under section 49B(6).

438. Paragraph 6 introduces new section 47C of the CA. Subsection (1) prohibits the CAT from awarding exemplary damages in collective proceedings, i.e. damages which are designed to be punitive rather than simply compensate for the actual loss suffered. This is to avoid very large damages being awarded which do not reflect the losses suffered. Subsection (2) enables the CAT to determine the damages due in collective proceedings without being required to consider each claim which forms part of the action. This is designed the avoid the CAT having to spend time assessing many individual claims and instead enables the CAT to group the claims together for the purpose of assessing damages. Subsection (5) provides that damages not claimed in opt-out collective proceedings must be paid to a charity specified by section 194(8) of the Legal Services Act 2007, unless under subsection (6) the Tribunal decides to award part or all of any unclaimed damages to the claimant's representative to cover their costs. Currently, the charity is the Access to Justice Foundation as recommended by the Jackson Review of Costs[48], the Civil Justice Council and HM Treasury's Financial Services Rules committee as a suitable body to receive unclaimed sums. Subsection (7) allows the Secretary of State to make regulations to substitute a different a different charity for one being prescribed at the time. Subsection (8) provides that damages-based agreements are not allowed in opt-out collective actions. A damages-based agreement is where some of the damages are paid to the legal representatives. Paragraph 37 amends section 58AA of the Courts and Legal Services Act 1990, to make clear this restriction on damages-based agreements applies, notwithstanding the other provisions of that Act.

439. Paragraph 25 amends Schedule 4 of the EA to allow representatives in a collective action to be able to take action to enforce an order concerning damages in collective proceedings.

440. Paragraph 26 replaces paragraph 6(a) and amends paragraph 6(b) of Schedule 4 EA to provide that where damages are awarded in a collective action to a person who is not a party to the order (i.e. they are not the representative or another person who the CAT considers are suitable to hold the damages and then distribute) or costs or expenses are awarded to a person in respect of a claim made under section 47A of the CA before

---

48 *Review of Civil Litigation Costs,* http://www.judiciary.gov.uk/NR/rdonlyres/8EB9F3F3-9C4A-4139-8A93-56F09672EB6A/0/jacksonfinalreport140110.pdf

it became part of the collective proceedings, it may only be enforced if permission is granted by the High Court or the Court of Session. This is to provide some judicial control over the volume of enforcement claims being made by persons who are not the representative or another person who the CAT considers is suitable to hold the damages.

441. Paragraph 27 amends paragraph 7 of Schedule 4 of the EA so that where any award of costs is made against a representative in collective proceedings, the person who is being represented (i.e. a particular business or consumer) may not be held responsible for those costs. This provision is designed to prevent legal costs being passed on from the representative to the persons who are being represented.

442. Paragraph 8 (see paragraph 428 above) introduces new section 47E of the CA which makes provisions about the limitation/prescription periods for claims before the CAT. Subsection (4) provides for there to be a suspension of the limitation/prescription period where claims are made under section 47B of the CA (collective proceedings). The purpose of this is to discourage parties from also commencing separate section 47A proceedings before the CAT, so as to protect their position. This is because the collective proceedings may only progress if a collective proceedings order is made. As this may not be made for some time, a party may be tempted to bring separate section 47A proceedings before the CAT to avoid the limitation/prescription period expiring before it knows whether the collective proceedings can be continued. The suspension of the limitation/prescription period offers protection to claimants who might otherwise be time-barred in bringing a single claim if the collective proceedings fail. Subsection (5) sets out when the limitation/prescription period will resume, such as where the Tribunal declines to make a collective proceedings order. Paragraph 29 replaces paragraph 11(2)(a) of Schedule 4 EA to enable rules to be made about the operation of the limitation and prescription periods.

443. The Government is also keen to encourage parties to settle disputes. To do this it is providing for collective settlements in opt-out collective proceedings where a collective proceedings order has been made as well as in cases where a collective proceedings order has not been made. The Government is also introducing voluntary redress schemes (see paragraphs 446 – 450 below). Paragraph 10 provides for a new section 49A of the CA which provides for collective settlements where a collective proceedings order has been made. Subsection (2) provides that the representative and the defendant must apply for approval of the proposed collective settlement. Subsection (4) provides that where there are multiple defendants, the defendants who want to be bound by an approved collective settlement must apply to the CAT. Subsection (5) provides that the CAT may approve the collective settlement if it is satisfied the terms are just and reasonable. Subsections (6) to (10) describes which persons are bound by the collective settlement.

444. Paragraph 11 introduces a new section 49B of the CA which enables a collective settlement to be made where a collective proceedings order has not been made. This procedure may be relevant if parties are at an early stage of the litigation. Subsection (4) requires that the CAT may only approve the collective settlement if it makes a collective settlement order. Subsection (5) provides that this requires the CAT to consider the person who proposes to be the settlement representative is a person who the CAT could approve as being a settlement representative and that if collective proceedings were brought, the claims would be suitable for inclusion in such proceedings. Subsection (8) provides the CAT may only approve the collective settlement if it considers its terms are just and reasonable. Subsections (9) and (10) provide for who is bound by a collective settlement order.

445. Paragraph 31 introduces paragraph 15C to Schedule 4 of the EA to provide that rules can be made about collective settlements. It also enables rules to be made to provide for costs to be paid by an underlying claimant who is not the representative in a collective action, in limited circumstances where he or she makes an application. For example, where a claimant makes an application to have their representative removed.

Voluntary redress schemes

446. The third aim is to define a voluntary redress scheme (referred to in legislation as a "redress scheme") so as to put it on a statutory footing. The government is keen for parties who are found liable for a breach of competition law to enter into negotiations with consumers or businesses where possible rather than the first route being a private action proceeding through the courts. The intention is to provide suitable, alternative mechanisms to allow for alternative dispute resolution. One mechanism is to allow the CMA to certify voluntary redress schemes that are entered into by businesses that have been found to have infringed competition law.

447. To support this goal, Government is introducing a new power enabling the CMA to certify redress schemes. Even without the certification, voluntary redress schemes can still be offered. However, Government wishes to place voluntary redress schemes on a firmer legal footing by allowing the CMA to approve binding, voluntary undertakings as to a compensation scheme. The intention would be that the CMA could take into account whether a business had bound themselves to provide redress when assessing the level of fine for the competition law breach.

448. Accordingly, paragraph 12 introduces new section 49C, which provides that the CMA may decide to approve a voluntary redress scheme (which may be put forward to the CMA prior to an infringement decision or after the decision has been made). Where a scheme is submitted prior to the CMA making an infringement decision, the CMA may approve an outline of the voluntary redress scheme, if it makes an infringement decision. The CMA may then require the business to create the full scheme afterwards which complies with any conditions imposed, such as the provision for further information by a set date. If the business does not comply with the conditions, the CMA may withdraw its approval of the voluntary redress scheme. Although the CMA will not determine the level of compensation that should be paid under the scheme, subsection (3) allows the CMA to take into account the amount or value of compensation when deciding whether or not to approve a voluntary redress scheme. This is to permit the CMA to reject a scheme, if the compensation on offer seems exceptionally low. Subsection (8) provides that the Secretary of State may make regulations about the approval of voluntary redress schemes. These regulations may make provisions about the procedure for approval, including the information to be provided. In addition, they may set out the factors the CMA should or should not take into account when considering applications for approval.

449. Paragraph 12 also inserts new section 49D to the CA. Section 49D provides that the CMA may require a person who applies for the approval of a voluntary redress scheme to pay the CMA's reasonable costs. The CMA will incur costs in considering an application for approval. In addition, paragraph 12 also inserts new section 49E to CA which provides in subsection (1) that a party who has a voluntary redress scheme approved has a duty to comply with its terms. Subsection (3) provides that if a business or consumer suffers as a result of a breach by a business of the terms of voluntary redress scheme, they may bring legal proceedings before a court for damages or another remedy, such as an injunction. This is to ensure there are remedies available for a breach of a voluntary redress scheme.

450. Paragraph 17 amends Schedule 8 of CA to allow for a business to appeal to the CAT against any costs imposed by the CMA in respect of a voluntary redress scheme.

Section 82: Appointment of Judges to the Competition Appeal Tribunal

451. This section changes the current process for appointing judges to the CAT to make it easier for judges from Scotland and Northern Ireland to be able to sit in the Tribunal as chairmen. It does this by providing for the Lord Chief Justices of England and Wales, and Northern Ireland and the Lord President of the Court of Session to be able to nominate judges sitting in their respective High Courts or the Court of Session for deployment as CAT chairmen.

452. Under the new provisions, the Lord Chief Justice of England and Wales will be able to nominate suitably qualified judges sitting in any Division of the High Court to be deployed as a judge in the CAT to sit as a chairman; currently, only judges appointed to the Chancery Division are appointed as CAT Chairs.

453. As a consequence of the change, the current eight year limit on appointment of judges in the CAT to sit as chairmen will not apply to those judges nominated to sit in the CAT and they will be able to sit until their retirement from the judiciary.

Chapter 3: Duty of Letting Agents to Publicise Fees Etc.

Summary and background

454. This Chapter imposes a duty on letting agents to publicise their fees, whether or not they are a member of a client money protection scheme and which redress scheme they have joined (fees etc). It explains which letting agents and which fees etc the duty applies to and details the enforcement of the duty.

455. Currently, although consumer rights legislation and guidance recommend that traders are clear and upfront about the fees which they charge, there is no specific duty for letting agents to display or publish their fees.

Section 83: Duty of letting agents to publicise fees etc

456. This section imposes a duty on letting agents to publicise 'relevant fees' (see commentary on section 85) and sets out how they must do this.

457. *Subsection (2)* requires agents to display a list of their fees at each of their premises where they deal face to face with customers and *subsection (3)* requires them to also publish a list of their fees on their website where they have a website.

458. *Subsection (4)* sets out what must be included in the list as follows. Subsection (4)(a) requires the fees to be described in such a way that a person who may have to pay the fee can understand what service or cost is covered by the fee or the reason why the fee is being imposed. For example, it will not be sufficient to call something an 'administration fee' without further describing what administrative costs or services that fee covers.

459. Subsection (4)(b) requires that where fees are charged to tenants the list should make clear whether the fee relates to each tenant under a tenancy or to the property. Finally, subsection (4)(c) requires the list to include the amount of each fee inclusive of tax, or, where the amount of the fee cannot be determined in advance a description of how that fee will be calculated. An example might be where a letting agent charges a landlord based on a percentage of rent.

460. *Subsection (6)* applies to letting agents who hold money on behalf of their clients as part of their letting agent or property management work. As well as publicising their fees, the agent must publish a statement which states whether or not that agent is a member of a client money protection scheme.

461. *Subsection (7)* means that agents who are required to belong to a redress scheme for dealing with complaints must publish which redress scheme they are a member of.

462. *Subsection (8)* enables the appropriate national authority to specify in regulations other ways in which letting agents must publicise details of their fees and the details that must be published. This could be used, for instance, to require letting agents to include information about fees in advertisements.

463. *Subsection (9)* defines a client money protection scheme and a redress scheme. A client money protection scheme is defined as a scheme which enables a client on whose behalf a letting agent holds money to be compensated by that scheme if all or part of that

money is not repaid in circumstances where the scheme applies. A redress scheme is defined as a scheme which has been approved by the Secretary of State by order under section 83 or 84 of the Enterprise and Regulatory Reform Act 2013.

Section 84: Letting agents to which the duty applies

464. This section defines who is a 'letting agent' and explains when someone who could be regarded as a letting agent is exempt from the requirements of this Chapter.

465. *Subsection (1)* defines a letting agent as someone who engages in 'letting agency work', which is defined in section 86.

466. *Subsection (2)* excludes a person who carries out letting agency work as part of their employment contract. This is to ensure that a salaried employee is not held responsible for publishing the fees.

467. *Subsection (3)* gives powers to the appropriate national authority to exclude other persons and activities in regulations.

Section 85: Fees to which the duty applies

468. This section defines 'relevant fees' for the purposes of the duty to publicise fees.

469. *Subsection (1)* provides that 'relevant fees' are the fees, charges or penalties which a landlord or tenant pays to the agent in relation to letting agency work, property management work or otherwise in connection with an assured tenancy or a dwelling-house let under an assured tenancy. *Subsection (2)* excludes certain payments from the definition of 'relevant fees'. Subsection (2)(a) excludes the rent payable to a landlord (many agents collect the rent on behalf of the landlord). Subsection (2)(b) excludes fees, charges or penalties which a landlord has to pay the agent but which the agent simply passes onto another person. For example, an agent may pay a gardener on behalf of a landlord and then reclaim this money from the landlord. Subsection (2)(c) excludes the deposit which is paid by the tenant in respect of the tenancy. Subsection (2)(d) gives the appropriate national authority the power to exclude other payments from the definition of 'relevant fees'.

Section 86: Letting agency work and property management work

470. This section defines letting agency work and property management work for the purposes of this Chapter.

471. *Subsection (1)* defines letting agency work as work undertaken on behalf of prospective landlords and prospective tenants and covers the process both of finding a tenant for the landlord or a property for a tenant and the work done to put the tenancy in place. It applies only to the letting of privately rented homes. *Subsection (2)* excludes from the definition of letting agency work those businesses that simply allow landlords and tenants to find and communicate with one another, provided they do not otherwise participate in the transaction.

472. *Subsection (3)* provides that local authorities are not included and thereby ensures that, for example, any local letting agency business established by local authorities is not caught by the duty in section 83.

473. *Subsection (4)* defines property management work for the purposes of this Chapter. The premises managed must consist of a dwelling-house let under an assured tenancy. As with letting agency work, property management work applies only to privately rented homes (see commentary on section 88 below).

*Section 87: **Enforcement of the duty***

474. *Subsection (1)* places a duty on every local weights and measures authority in England and Wales to enforce the requirement for letting agents to publicise their fees etc in its area.

475. *Subsection (2)* sets out that, if an agent breaches the duty in section 83(3) to publicise fees on its website, that breach is taken to have occurred in the area in which the property to which the fees relate is located.

476. *Subsection (3)* enables local weights and measures authorities who are satisfied on the balance of probabilities that a letting agent has breached the requirement to impose a financial penalty on the agent in respect of that breach.

477. *Subsection (4)* provides that while it is the duty of local weights and measures authorities to enforce the requirement in their area, they may also impose a penalty in respect of a breach which occurs in England and Wales but outside that authority's area. However, *subsection (6)* ensures that an agent may only be fined once in respect of the same breach.

478. *Subsection (5)* requires a local weights and measures authority who wants to impose a fine in respect of a breach outside its own area but in the area of a Welsh authority, to seek the consent of that authority.

479. *Subsection (7)* provides that local weights and measures authorities may fine letting agents in breach of the requirement up to £5,000. When imposing a fine, *subsection (8)* states that authorities must follow the process described in Schedule 9.

480. *Subsection (9)* requires a local weights and measures authority in England to have regard to any guidance issued by the Secretary of State about how letting agents should comply with the duty to publicise their fees etc and on how the authority should carry out its enforcement duties.

481. Similarly *subsection (10)* requires a local weights and measures authority in Wales to have regard to any guidance issued by the Welsh Ministers about how letting agents should comply with the duty to publicise their fees etc and on how the authority should carry out its enforcement duties.

482. *Subsection (11) and (12)* give both the Secretary of State and the Welsh Ministers the power to make secondary legislation which amends the enforcement provisions and make the necessary consequential amendments for England and Wales respectively.

*Section 88: **Supplementary provisions***

483. *Subsections (1) to (4)* provide the remaining definitions of the terms used in this Chapter. The definition of an assured tenancy is relevant to determining firstly who is a letting agent for the purposes of this Chapter and, secondly, the fees to which the duty applies. *Subsection (1)* defines an assured tenancy (which is the most common type of tenancy in the private rented sector) for these purposes. In particular, the definition of an assured tenancy excludes assured tenancies granted by a private registered provider of social housing and any assured tenancy that is a long lease. This ensures that the duty applies to agents who let properties in the private rented sector and to the fees, penalties and charges that they charge in connection with the letting, management etc. of such properties.

484. *Subsections (5) to (9)* set out the Parliamentary procedures for making the regulations detailed in this Chapter and *subsections (10) and (11)* provide a power for incidental provision to be made.

Chapter 4: Student Complaints Scheme

Section 89: Qualifying Institutions for the purposes of the student complaints scheme

485. The section expands the list of higher education providers which are required to join the higher education complaints handling scheme. All those delivering courses which are specifically or automatically designated to receive student support funding in England and Wales and providers with degree awarding powers will be required to join. This scheme was set up under the provisions of the Higher Education Act 2004 and is operated by the Office of the Independent Adjudicator for Higher Education.

Chapter 5: Secondary Ticketing

Summary and Background

486. This Chapter concerns the online secondary ticketing market. That is, the market where tickets for sporting, recreational and cultural events are re-sold having been first bought or otherwise acquired on the primary market from an event organiser. It concerns:

- Information which must be provided in respect of a ticket to its buyer, when that ticket is resold online;
- The original terms and conditions of a ticket;
- Reporting of criminal activity on online ticket marketplaces; and
- A review of the online secondary ticketing market.

487. Currently, there are no provisions in statute specifically regulating the online secondary ticketing market. There is, however, other legislation which applies generally and in so doing covers the market, including:

- The Consumer Contracts (Information, Cancellation and Additional Charges) Regulations 2013 (SI 2013/3134) which provide that certain information must be provided when goods, a service or digital content are sold by a trader to a consumer, including sales concluded at a distance (e.g. online);
- Section 166 of the Criminal Justice and Public Order Act 1994 which regulates the re-selling of tickets for certain football matches;
- The Fraud Act 2006 and the Consumer Protection from Unfair Trading Regulations 2008 (SI 2008/1277) which aim to protect buyers from misleading or fraudulent sales; and
- The Unfair Terms in Consumer Contracts Regulations 1999 (SI 1999/2083) (which are to be replaced by Part 2 of the Act once Part 2 comes into force) which provide that terms in a consumer contract must be fair.

488. This Chapter applies to tickets for all recreational, sporting and cultural events taking place in the UK[49].

Duty to provide information about tickets

Section 90: Duty to provide information about tickets

489. Section 90 sets out the information which is to be provided when a ticket is re-sold online by virtue of these provisions. As noted above, additional statutory information requirements may also apply. This section applies when a ticket is re-sold through an

49 This Chapter is, however, without prejudice to any existing restrictions on the resale of tickets, such as that set out in section 166 Criminal Justice and Public Order Act 1994.

online secondary ticketing facility. This might be a website but could equally be a web based application (or other type of online facility). This section applies to tickets first offered for re-sale after the entry into force of the section.

490. The duty to provide information rests on both the seller of the ticket and the person operating the online facility through which it is being sold. In practice, it will be for the seller to give the information when they go to list their tickets online, and for the operator then to ensure that this information is given to the buyer.

491. There are four pieces of information which must be given. *Firstly, subsection (3)(a)* requires information to enable the buyer to identify the particular seat or standing area of the venue to which the ticket applies. This includes, where applicable, the name of the relevant area of the venue, the block in which the seat or relevant area is located, and the row and number of the seat. Where the seat and row are identified by something other than a number, this identifier must also be given.

492. Secondly, under *subsection (3)(b)* the buyer must be given information about any restrictions that apply to the ticket and concern who can use it. For example, the ticket might be for a specific area reserved for disabled persons, or it might only be able to be used by those under 12 years old.

493. Thirdly, *subsection (3)(c)* requires the face value of the ticket to be given. This is the price printed on the ticket itself. This will likely be the price at which the seller originally bought the ticket for.

494. Fourthly, where the seller has a connection with the online facility on which they are selling, or the organiser of the event for which the ticket is being sold, under *subsection (6)* they must state that this is the case, and what that connection is. For example, if the seller is an employee of the facility which they are using to sell the tickets, they must give the buyer that information. Where the seller is the operator of the facility itself, this information must be given.

495. In each case, the seller only has to provide this information where it is applicable to them or the ticket they are selling. For example, where a ticket is for a standing section of a venue, the seller does not have to give a seat number. The seller must make reasonable attempts to obtain and then provide this information to the buyer, however it is acknowledged that there are circumstances where this might not be possible, such as where the ticket is resold before the event organiser has allocated seat numbers.

496. *Subsection (8)* requires the information to be provided in a clear and comprehensible manner, and before the buyer purchases the ticket. For example, the information would be clearly displayed in a legible font before the buyer clicks on a button marked "confirm purchase".

Section 91: ***Prohibition on cancellation or blacklisting***

497. Section 91 sites alongside section 90 and provides for consumer protections when the information required by section 90 is given. Information provided under section 90 could be used by an event organiser to cancel a ticket or blacklist a seller. An event organiser may also seek to cancel a ticket or blacklist a seller for other reasons or based on other information.

498. Section 91 provides that an event organiser cannot cancel a ticket (*subsection (2)*) or blacklist a seller (*subsection (3)*) merely because that ticket is resold or offered for resale unless two conditions are met:

499. Firstly, it must be a term of the contract under which the original buyer purchased the ticket from the event organiser that cancellation of the ticket and/or blacklisting of the seller may occur as a consequence of that ticket being resold or offered for resale.

500. Secondly, that term of the contract under which the original buyer purchased the ticket from the event organiser must not be unfair. The fairness of terms in consumer contracts is assessable under Part 2 of this Act (see paragraphs 287 to 348 of these notes) and, before the coming into force of those provisions, under the Unfair Terms in Consumer Contracts Regulations 1999. Unfair terms are not enforceable against consumers.

501. Blacklisting of a seller includes not just the placing of the seller on a list of those sellers who cannot, or cannot without restriction, purchase further tickets. Blacklisting covers any steps taken by an event organiser to prevent or restrict that seller buying tickets, in any form.

502. *Subsection (9)* applies this prohibition to actions taken by event organisers after this section comes into force. The ticket in question may have, however, been resold or offered for resale before that time.

Section 92: Duty to report criminal activity

503. This section provides that, where the operator of a secondary ticketing facility is aware of criminal activity on that facility, a relevant report must be made to the police and to the event organiser. This section applies to criminal activity related to the resale of tickets (though there may be other reporting requirements which apply where this is not the case).

504. Criminal activity means where an offence is committed, under the law of any part of the UK. There are several pieces of legislation breach of which could lead to an offence being committed. However this provision is intended to cover legislation for which the authorities listed here (that is, the police) are one of the principal enforcers. This includes offences under the Fraud Act 2006 and the Theft Act 1968.

505. *Subsection (3)* specifies that the information to be reported is—where this is known to the operator—the identity of the person committing the offence (for example their company name or an individual's name) and the fact that the operator knows that a criminal offence is or has been committed.

506. The report must be made to a police force within the United Kingdom. Where, for example, the facility is aware that the person is based in England the report could be made to a police constable in England. Where there is a lead police force for a particular crime (for example fraud) that force might be the appropriate police force to which the report can be made. A report must also be made to the organiser of the relevant event(s), that is, where the criminal activity involves tickets for a particular event, the organiser of that event must be informed. However, under *subsection (5)* such a report is not required if it would prejudice the investigation of an offence (not just the one being reported). In practice, this might mean that—where the facility has some doubt —the report is first made to the police who can advise whether a report to an event organiser would prejudice an investigation.

507. The criminal activity can be either ongoing or have already occurred, however the operator of the facility need only report offences which it became aware of after this provision comes into force.

Section 93: Enforcement of this Chapter

508. This section provides for enforcement of sections 90, 91 and 92. Enforcement is by local weights and measures authorities in Great Britain (known as Trading Standards) and by the Department of Enterprise, Trade and Investment in Northern Ireland.

509. *Subsection (4)* allows these enforcers to levy a fine of up to £5000 for a breach of the requirements in those sections. That fine can be levied on a private individual or a business, depending on the nature of the breach.

510. This sanction is, however, limited by *subsection (5)* which states that an enforcer may not impose a fine for a breach of the duty in section 90 or the prohibition in section 91 if it is satisfied that the breach was the result of circumstances beyond a person's control, for example a mistake or accident, and the person had taken reasonable precautions and undertaken due diligence. For example, where an online ticket marketplace had been supplied with false information by a seller, and had taken reasonable steps to ensure that that information was correct, they would not be liable for a fine.

511. This section also gives effect to Schedule 10 (secondary ticketing: financial penalties) which provides for the procedure to be followed when enforcing the provisions in this Chapter:

a) Before a fine is levied, paragraph 1 of this Schedule requires a relevant enforcer to give a notice of intent. This must be given within 6 months of the enforcer having evidence of a breach. Within 28 days of receiving that notice, the person on whom it is served can make representations. Once the 28 day period has expired, the enforcer can issue a final notice giving details of the level of the fine and how it is to be paid. The notice can be withdrawn at any time.

b) Once a final notice has been issued, the person on whom it is served can appeal on the grounds given in paragraph 5 of this Schedule.

c) Should the final notice not be appealed, or be upheld on appeal, and the fine not be paid, the enforcer can ask the county court (or in Scotland, a sheriff court) for an order to recover that fine under paragraph 6 of this Schedule.

*Section 94: **Duty to review measures relating to secondary ticketing***

512. This section provides for a review of the online secondary ticketing market. The review must either be carried out by the Secretary of State or arranged by the Secretary of State to be carried out, *e.g.* by an external reviewer.

513. The review:

a) must cover the online secondary ticketing market for recreational, sporting and cultural events in the UK;

b) must cover consumer protection measures in the secondary market, defined as such legislation, rules of law, codes of practice and guidance which the Secretary of State deems relevant;

c) must prepare and publish a report within 12 months of this section coming into force; and

d) must be presented to Parliament.

*Section 95: **Interpretation of this Chapter***

514. This section gives the definitions that apply to terms used in this Chapter. It includes a power for the Secretary of State to change by regulations who this Chapter applies to through changing the definition of the operator of a secondary ticketing facility.

COMMENCEMENT

515. The provisions of the Act listed in section 100(2) come into force on the day of Royal Assent. For the most part these are powers to make secondary legislation, but the general provisions in Chapter 6 of Part 3 also come into force on Royal Asset. Chapter 5 of Part 3 comes into force at the end of the period of two months beginning with the day of Royal Assent.

516. The remaining provisions of this Act, apart from Chapters 3 and 4 of Part 3, will come into force on such day as the Secretary of State may appoint by order made by Statutory

Instrument. Chapters 3 and 4 will be brought into force by the Secretary of State in relation to England and the Welsh Ministers in relation to Wales. Different days may be appointed for different purposes.

HANSARD REFERENCE

517. The following table sets out the dates and Hansard reference for each stage of this Act's passage through Parliament. Links to the Hansard extracts can be found here: http://services.parliament.uk/bills/2014-15/consumerrights/stages.html

Stage	***Date***	***Hansard reference***
House of Commons		
Introduction	23 January 2014	Vol 574; Col 478
Second Reading	28 January 2014	Vol 574; Col 768
Public Bill Committee on the Consumer Rights Bill	11 February 2014	Morning: Col 3-38
		Afternoon: Col 41-77
	13 February 2014	Morning: Col 81-106
		Afternoon: Col 109-162
	25 February 2014	Morning: Col 165-208
		Afternoon: Col 211-266
	27 February 2014	Morning: Col 269-294
		Afternoon: Col 297-336
	4 March 2014	Morning: Col 339-380
		Afternoon: Col 383-446
	6 March 2014	Morning: Col 449-474
		Afternoon: Col 477-525
	11 March 2014	Morning: Col 529-572
		Afternoon: Col 575-628
	13 March 2014	Col 631-658
Report and Third Reading	13 May 2014 (1st day)	Vol 580; Col 600
	16 June 2014 (2nd day)	Vol 582; Col 873
	16 June 2014 (3rd Reading)	Vol 582; Col 915
House of Lords		
Introduction	17 June 2014	Vol 754; Col 764
Second Reading	1 July 2014	Vol 754; Col 1645
Committee	13 October 2014	Vol 756; GC1
	15 October 2014	Vol 756; GC99
	20 October 2014	Vol 756; GC163
	22 October 2014	Vol 756; GC215
	27 October 2014	Vol 756; GC307

Stage	***Date***	***Hansard reference***
	29 October 2014	Vol 756; GC441
	3 November 2014	Vol 756; GC561
	5 November 2014	Vol 756; GC689
Report	19 November 2014	Vol 757; Col 455
	24 November 2014	Vol 757; Col 701
	26 November 2014	Vol 757; Col 890
Third Reading	8 December 2014	Vol 757; Col 1601
Ping Pong		
Commons Consideration of Lords Amendments	12 January 2015	Vol 590; Col 625
Lords Consideration of Commons Reason	24 February 2015	Vol 759; Col 1539
Commons Consideration of Lords Non-Instance and Amendments in Lieu	9 March 2015	Vol 594; Col 55
Royal Assent		
Commons	26 March 2015	Vol 594; Col 1682
Lords	26 March 2015	Vol 760; Col 1589

ANNEX A: GLOSSARY OF ABBREVIATIONS

2013 Regulations	Consumer Contracts (Information, Cancellation and Additional Charges) Regulations 2013
ADR	Alternative Dispute Resolution
BIS	Department for Business, Innovation and Skills
CA	Competition Act 1998
CAA	Civil Aviation Authority
CAT	Competition Appeal Tribunal
CMA	Competition and Markets Authority
CPRs	Consumer Protection from Unfair Trading Regulations 2008
CRD	Consumer Rights Directive (Directive 2011/83/EU of the European Parliament and of the Council on consumer rights)
CSD	Consumer Sales Directive (Directive 1999/44/EC of the European Parliament and Council on certain aspects of the sale of consumer goods and associated guarantees)
EA	Enterprise Act 2002
ECHR	European Convention on Human Rights
EEA	European Economic Area
EU	European Union
EUCJ	European Union Court of Justice
IA	Impact Assessment
ISP	Internet Service Provider
NIAUR	Northern Ireland Authority for Utility Regulation
Ofcom	The Office of Communications
Ofgem	The Office of Gas and Electricity Markets
OFT	Office of Fair Trading
Ofwat	The Water Service Regulation Authority
ORR	Office of the Rail Regulator
SGA	Sale of Goods Act 1979
SGITA	Supply of Goods (Implied Terms) Act 1973
SGSA	Supply of Goods and Services Act 1982
SME	Small and medium sized enterprise
TFEU	Treaty on the Functioning of the European Union
UCTA	Unfair Contract Terms Act 1977

UTCCD	Unfair Terms in Consumer Contracts Directive (Council Directive 1993/13/EEC on unfair terms in consumer contracts)
UTCCRs	The Unfair Terms in Consumer Contract Regulations 1999

ANNEX B: TRANSPOSITION NOTES

DIRECTIVE OF THE EUROPEAN PARLIAMENT AND OF THE COUNCIL 1999/44/EC OF 25 MAY 1999 ON CERTAIN ASPECTS OF THE SALE OF CONSUMER GOODS AND ASSOCIATED GUARANTEES

518. This note describes the implementation in the Consumer Rights Act 2015 of Directive 1999/44/EC of the European Parliament and of the Council of 25 May 1999 on certain aspects of the sale of consumer goods and associated guarantees.[50] The Directive requires that goods sold to consumers must be in conformity with the contract and consumers have certain remedies if goods are not in conformity with the contract. The Directive also requires that guarantees provided free of charge alongside goods be legally binding.

519. The deadline for implementing the Directive passed on 1 January 2002. The legislation currently implementing the Directive can be found in the Sale and Supply of Goods to Consumers Regulations 2002 (SI 2002/3045) and in the Sale of Goods Act 1979, the Supply of Goods and Services Act 1982 and the Supply of Goods (Implied Terms) Act 1973 each of which SI 2002/3045 amended. The Consumer Rights Act 2015 repeals and replaces the provisions of those pieces of legislation which currently implement the Directive.

520. UK law has long provided that goods must meet certain requirements, which are implied into contracts for goods, and consumers have remedies if the requirements are not met. The Directive was implemented by amending and supplementing pre-existing law. The Act goes beyond the minimum requirements of the Directive in a number of respects, as it reflects both the Directive and embedded UK law.

521. The table below describes the main substantive provisions of the Act implementing the Directive.

DIRECTIVE 1999/44/EC ON CERTAIN ASPECTS OF THE SALE OF CONSUMER GOODS AND ASSOCIATED GUARANTEES

Article	*Objective*	*Implementation*
1.1	Includes scope of application.	Section 3
1.2	Definitions of key terms.	Definitions for the Act are set out in sections 2 and 59 and include definitions which adequately implement the terms defined by the Directive. Section 23 contains the definition of 'repair'. Section 30 contains the definition of 'guarantee' and other terms used in that section.
2.1-2.3	Goods to conform with the contract for sale.	Sections 9, 10, 11, 13 and 14; section 19(1)
2.4	Circumstances where the seller is not to be bound by public statements about the goods.	Section 9(7)
2.5	Lack of conformity resulting from incorrect installation of the consumer goods to be deemed to be equivalent to lack of conformity of the goods.	Section 15

50 OJ L 171, 7/7/1999, p.12.

Article	*Objective*	*Implementation*
3.1-3.5	Seller to be liable to the consumer for any lack of conformity which exists at the time the goods were delivered, and to make specified remedies available to the consumer, as follows: (i) Repair or replacement, in either case free of charge, unless impossible or disproportionate; (ii) Appropriate reduction of the price or rescission of the contract, if the consumer is entitled to neither repair nor replacement, or the seller has not provided repair or replacement within a reasonable time or without significant inconvenience to the consumer.	Sections 19, 23, 24
3.6	Rescission unavailable if lack of conformity is minor.	Not implemented in the UK
4	Right of redress for seller as against persons liable to the seller in the contractual chain.	No change to UK law is required to implement Article 4
5.1	Seller to be held liable where the lack of conformity becomes apparent within two years as from delivery of the goods.	No change to UK law is required to implement Article 5.1. The UK relies instead on its pre-existing rules on limitation of actions.
5.2	Consumers may be required to notify the seller of a lack of conformity with 2 months of its appearance.	Not implemented in the UK
5.3	Lack of conformity appearing within first 6 months to be deemed to have been present at time of deliver unless proven otherwise.	Section 19(14) – (15)
6	Guarantees.	Section 30
7.1	Contractual terms which waive the rights under the Directive are not to be binding.	Section 31
7.2	Choice of law of a non-EU State not to deprive consumer of protection.	Section 32
8	Rights under the Directive to be exercised without prejudice to national law. Option to maintain stricter national legislation.	As explained above, the Directive has been implemented within pre-existing UK rules.

COUNCIL DIRECTIVE 93/13/EEC OF 5 APRIL 1993 ON UNFAIR TERMS IN CONSUMER CONTRACTS

522. This note describes the implementation in the Consumer Rights Act 2015 of Council Directive 93/13/EEC of 5 April 1993 on unfair terms in consumer contracts.[51] The Directive requires that unfair terms in contracts concluded between a trader and a consumer are not binding.

523. The deadline for implementing the Directive passed on 31 December 1994. The legislation currently implementing the Directive can be found in the Unfair Terms in Consumer Contracts Regulations 1999 (SI 1999/2083). The Consumer Rights Act 2015 repeals and replaces the provisions of those Regulations.

524. The Act goes beyond the minimum requirements of the Directive in a number of respects:

- application to all consumer contract terms, whether or not individually negotiated;
- application to trader's notices directed at consumers, whether or not incorporated in a consumer contract;
- contracts and notices excluding trader's liability in negligence for death or personal injury are not binding;
- terms on main subject matter and price are exempt from assessment of fairness only if transparent and prominent;
- three further terms added to 'grey list'.

525. The table below describes the main substantive provisions of the Act implementing the Directive.

DIRECTIVE 93/13/EEC ON UNFAIR TERMS IN CONSUMER CONTRACTS: TRANSPOSITION MEASURES

Article	*Objective*	*Implementation*
1.1	Defines scope of application	Section 61
1.2	Exclusion of mandatory statutory provisions	Section 73
2	Definitions of key terms	Sections 61, 76 and 2
3.1	Fairness test	Section 62
3.2	Terms not regarded as individually negotiated	No implementation required (section 61 applies to terms whether individually negotiated or not).
3.3	Indicative and non-exhaustive 'grey list' of terms that may be unfair, as set out in Annex to Directive	Section 63 and Schedule 2
4.1	Circumstances to consider in assessing fairness.	Section 62
4.2	Exception from fairness assessment for terms on main subject matter and price	Section 64

51 OJ L 95, 21/04/1993, p.29.

Article	*Objective*	*Implementation*
5	Terms to be in plain and intelligible language	Sections 68 and 69
6.1	Unfair terms not to be binding	Sections 62(1), 67 and 72
6.2	Choice of law of a non-EU State not to deprive consumer of protection	Section 74
7	Effective enforcement	Section 70 and Schedule 3; Part 3 of Schedule 5 in addition to enforcement by public bodies under Part 8 of the Enterprise Act 2002, and private actions brought by individuals.
8	Option to retain stricter national legislation	See paragraph 524 above.
9	Commission review of Directive	No implementation required.
10	Implementation by 31 December 1994	No implementation required in Act.
11	Directive addressed to Member States	No implementation required.

DIRECTIVE 2011/83/EU OF THE EUROPEAN PARLIAMENT AND OF THE COUNCIL ON CONSUMER RIGHTS

526. This note describes the implementation in the Consumer Rights Act 2015 of Directive 2011/83/EU of the European Parliament and of the Council of 25 October 2011 on consumer rights, amending Council Directive 93/13/EEC and Directive 1999/44/EC of the European Parliament and of the Council and repealing Council Directive 85/577/EEC and Directive 97/7/EC of the European Parliament and of the Council.

527. The Directive covers

- Information which traders should provide to consumers
- Cancellation rights and responsibilities for distance and off-premises sales
- Delivery and passing of risk provisions
- Measures to prevent hidden costs

528. The regulations that, alongside the Consumer Rights Act 2015, implement the Directive can be found in the Consumer Contracts (Information, Cancellation and Additional Charges) Regulations 2013 (SI 2013/3134). A full transposition note for the Directive was published alongside the regulations and can be found at www.gov.uk/bis. The Act replaces a small number of provisions of these Regulations, as set out below, for coherence with related measures in the Act, in accordance with the Government's aim to ensure that regulation is simple and coherent as possible.

529. The provisions in the Act listed below reflect those in the Directive.

530. The two areas implemented in the Act relate to pre-contractual information and to the delivery of goods and passing of risk. Pre-contractual information, is made a term of the contract. In addition, the Act implements rules for the timing of delivery for goods and regarding when responsibility transfers from the trader to the consumer for goods delivered. The table below describes the transposition in the Act of the relevant provisions of the Directive.

Article	***Objective***	***Implementation***
PRE-CONTRACTUAL INFORMATION		
6.5	Information provided to be incorporated into contract	Sections 11(4)-(6), 12, 36(3)-(4), 37 50(3)-(4)
DELIVERY OF GOODS AND PASSING OF RISK		
17.1	Scope of application of Articles 18 and 20, to sales contracts only.	Sections 5, 28(1) and 29(1)
18.1	Default rule for sales contracts of delivery within 30 days	Section 28(3)
18.2	If late delivery, consumer to nominate a further delivery period. Consumer may terminate contract if second failure.	Section 28(5)-(8)
18.3	Trader to reimburse all payments to consumer on termination	Section 28(9)-(10)
18.4	Consumer may have other remedies in national law	Section 28(10)-(13)
20	For sales contracts, risk of loss or damage passes to consumer when consumer acquires possession of goods	Section 29
GENERAL PROVISIONS		
23.1	Adequate and effective enforcement	In relation to the provisions above, sections 11(4)-(6), 12, 19, 28, 36(3)-(4), 37, 38, 42, 50 and 54 of the Consumer Rights Act 2015. A future Order providing that the regime under Part 8 of the Enterprise Act 2002 for public bodies and consumer bodies to enforce consumer law applies in relation to the relevant provisions of the Act.
24.1	Effective, proportionate and dissuasive penalties for enforcement.	In relation to the provisions above, sections 11(4)-(6), 12, 19, 28, 36(3)-(4), 37, 38, 42, 50 and 54 of the Consumer Rights Act 2015. A future Order providing that the regime under Part 8 of the Enterprise Act 2002 for public bodies and consumer bodies to enforce consumer law applies in relation to the relevant provisions of the Act

DIRECTIVES CONFERRING EFFECTIVE ENFORCEMENT MEASURES

531. This note describes how the Consumer Rights Act 2015 gives effect to key Directives that require effective enforcement measures to be implemented with regard to consumer law.

532. These include Directive 2005/29/EC of 11 May 2005 concerning unfair business-to-consumer commercial practices in the internal market[52]; Directive 2006/114/EC of the European Parliament and of the Council of 12 December 2006 concerning misleading and comparative advertising[53]; Directive 2001/95/EC of the European Parliament and of the Council of 3 December 2001 on General Product Safety[54]; Directive 2004/22/EC of the European Parliament and of the Council of 31 March 2004 on measuring instruments[55]; and Council Directive 76/211/EEC of 20 January 1976 on the approximation of the laws of the Member States relating to the making-up by weight or by volume of certain prepackaged products.[56]

533. The tables below describe how the provisions of the Act implement these key Directives.

COUNCIL DIRECTIVE 76/211/EEC ON THE APPROXIMATION OF THE LAWS OF THE MEMBER STATES RELATING TO THE MAKING-UP BY WEIGHT OR BY VOLUME OF CERTAIN PRE-PACKAGED PRODUCTS

Article	*Objective*	*Implementation*
Annex I, Paragraphs 5 - 6	Establishes the conformity assessment of measuring instruments by competent authorities to ensure the instruments are correct and traceable for the purposes of fair trading and protecting the consumer.	Parts 3 and 4 of Schedule 5 confer powers in relation to civil and criminal enforcement.

COUNCIL DIRECTIVE 2001/95/EEC ON GENERAL PRODUCT SAFETY

Article	*Objective*	*Implementation*
8.1	Establishes the principal measures that competent authorities are to be able to take in respect of unsafe products, including the obtaining of information and samples.	Parts 3 and 4 of Schedule 5 confer powers in relation to civil and criminal enforcement.

DIRECTIVE 2004/22/EC ON MEASURING INSTRUMENTS

Article	*Objective*	*Implementation*
18.1	Requires Member States to take all appropriate measures to ensure that measuring instruments that are subject to legal metrological control but do not comply with an	Parts 3 and 4 of Schedule 5 confer powers in relation to civil and criminal enforcement.

52 Amending Directives 84/450/EEC, 97/7/EC, 98/27/EC and 2002/65/EC and Regulation (EC) No 2006/2004 (Unfair Commercial Practices Directive), OJ L 149, 11.6.2005

53 OJ L 376, 27/12/2006

54 OJ L 11, 15/01/2002

55 OJ L 135, 30/04/2004

56 OJ L 46, 21/2/1976

Article	Objective	Implementation
	applicable provision of the Directive are neither placed on the market nor put into use.	

DIRECTIVE 2005/29/EC CONCERNING UNFAIR BUSINESS-TO-CONSUMER COMMERCIAL PRACTICES IN THE INTERNAL MARKET

Article	Objective	Implementation
11.1, paragraph 1	Requires Member States to ensure that adequate and effective means exist to combat unfair commercial practice in order to enforce the Directive.	Parts 3 and 4 of Schedule 5 confer powers in relation to civil and criminal enforcement.

DIRECTIVE 2006/114/EC CONCERNING MISLEADING AND COMPARATIVE ADVERTISING

Article	Objective	Implementation
5.1, paragraph 1	Requires Member States to ensure that adequate and effective means exist to combat misleading advertising and enforce compliance with the provisions on comparative advertising in the interests of traders and competitors.	Parts 3 and 4 of Schedule 5 confer powers in relation to civil and criminal enforcement.

Adapted and published by GRANGIS under the OGL Licence 3.0.

www.nationalarchives.gov.uk/doc/open-government-licence/version/3/

GRANGIS - UK PUBLISHING 2022.

Thank you for taking the time to leave us a review regarding this version

★★★★★

For further inquiries, contact us at:
www.grangis.com / contact@grangis.com

www.ingramcontent.com/pod-product-compliance
Lightning Source LLC
LaVergne TN
LVHW060213210926
848481LV00008B/2725